I0460231

I, SEAN/A

The Story Of A Homeless Intersex Woman Who Inspired A Community

Dr. Kirsten Viola Harrison
With Sean/a Smith

Copyright © 2025 Kirsten Viola Harrison & Sean/a Smith

ALL RIGHTS RESERVED
No part of this book may be translated, used, or reproduced in any form or by any means, in whole or in part, electronic or mechanical, including photocopying, recording, taping, or by any information storage or retrieval system without express written permission from the author or the publisher, except for the use in brief quotations within critical articles and reviews.

(soulwiseteam@gmail.com)

Limits of Liability:
The authors and/or publisher shall not be liable for your misuse of this material. The contents are strictly for informational and educational purposes only.

Disclaimer:
The purpose of this book is to educate and entertain. The authors and/or publisher do not guarantee that anyone following these techniques, suggestions, tips, ideas, or strategies will become successful. The author and/or publisher shall have neither liability nor responsibility to anyone with respect to any loss or damage caused, or alleged to be caused, directly or indirectly by the information contained in this book.

Cover photos by Kim Utley. Other photos by Kim Utley can be found on pages 6, 8, 98, 111, 145, 182, 194, 214, 228, 230, 240, 242, 261, 262, 291, 316, 326, 337.

Introduction photo by Kim Hoffman. Other photos by Kim Hoffman can be found on pages 10, 25, 38, 39, 68, 152, 164, 165, 181, 195, 196, 213, 240, 260.

Cover and interior design by Stefan Merour

Printed and bound in the United States of America
ISBNs:
Paperback: 979-8-9905330-0-4
Hardcover: 979-8-9905330-1-1
Ebook: 979-8-9905330-2-8

DEDICATION

To my family for instilling in me and demonstrating a deep and abiding love of humanity. For the joy of my life, my daughter Tia, may you continue to dwell in possibility.

For Sean/a, who has always given far more than she has received.

~KVH

To anyone who thinks life is not worth living, IT IS.

~Sean/a

CONTENTS

INTRODUCTION

"The chance to have this book written 📖 and to recover some of the things 🔍 🚢 that were lost over the years has restored my dignity. It's like being on a ship out to sea and capsizing. You have a life preserver, but you lose all your valuables... Years later you get back the items that drifted ashore that truly belonged to you."

—Sean/a

Many have asked what my relationship with Sean/a has been like. Although it has changed over the years, it began as a simple offering of compassion, one human being to another. It evolved into a series of brief conversations about Sean/a's well-being, at which time I learned about her homelessness and grew concerned for her welfare.

Over time, our relationship has progressed to a philosophical journey of sorts. Amidst our random musings about life, I have come to understand portions of Sean/a's history. The two of us have become friends and co-creators of a new life in which Sean/a thrives and feels safe, off the streets.

Even though Sean/a calls me "Doc," she has never been a patient of mine. Any "street therapy" has always been from the perspective of friendly, informal life coaching. Along the way, we've created plans and strategies for Sean/a's long-term success.

1

Sometimes the two of us operate in a mentor-learner type of connection, but we are constantly taking turns at who is the mentor and who is the learner. At other times, we feel like deeply connected team members trying to understand life's lessons, hopefully relating those truths for others to be inspired by her journey.

In writing this book with Sean/a, I have felt the need to maintain an awareness that seemingly innocuous details can be triggering or cause distress. The clinician in me has been ever cognizant of this potential risk. Inherent safeguards we have built into this process are the longstanding, faithful, and solid friendship Sean/a and I share. I can only be grateful that she has entrusted me with such intimate details of her life.

Sean/a has been very open and public about her life's story in order that she may guide others by example, through her lived experience. I am just one of many with whom she has shared her trials and tribulations—and ultimately, her triumphs. There has been no obligation or coercion inherent in this project.

Much of Sean/a's personal backstory is ambiguous. Despite our close relationship, she has been reluctant to share many details about her family and childhood, and I have respected her approach and right to privacy in this. How much or little she revealed was up to her level of comfort and what she deemed important to share.

We all have spaces in our lives where we would hesitate to shine a light and reveal the most personal aspects. Sean/a stated, "A wise senior college pastor of mine taught me that 'you don't give everything away, you have to keep some things to yourself.' Discretion, privacy, and emotional support, and most importantly dignity and respect … those are yours." It's a balancing act.

When writing this story—with the camera angle focused on a life that is not my own—I share what Sean/a is willing to share, respecting her integrity and personal space. I remain silent or skip past those spaces she would prefer to keep to herself, not intruding too deeply. I trust you'll understand and respect this approach.

One aim of this work is to make sure Sean/a has the ability to live the life she has imagined, a life of acceptance and belonging, free from harm and with the secure knowledge that she will not ever need to return to homelessness. We hope that her story paves the way for those who have yet to understand their own personal power in their respective journeys toward wholeness.

Another goal we have had is to facilitate positive change—specifically in highlighting the myriad issues Sean/a has faced throughout her life: a complicated childhood, years on the streets, racial discrimination, mental distress, and living as an intersex individual long before anyone understood, much less accepted, the term. These are topics we unpack throughout the pages of this book.

Sean/a is the "poster child" for rising above adversity. Through countless setbacks, she has shown tremendous resilience and never lost her spiritual center. In fact, she has used this internal compass to direct herself through dark spaces. I believe that ineffable center, that spiritual navigation, has the potential to guide us all.

I have been very blessed to have Sean/a in my life and I hope, by the time you finish reading this book, you will feel touched by a little of her spirit in these pages. It has been a challenge not to get ahead of myself while writing these chapters, as I'm wildly enthusiastic about the way Sean/a enriches those around her with that remarkable flair and her unabashed desire to stay true to herself.

Even while facing housing insecurity and financial hardship, Sean/a was never too tired or overwhelmed to share her heart and positivity with others. Her zest for life under all kinds of circumstances has modeled to me what resilience and post-traumatic growth look like.

Sean/a has never shied away from controversy. Instead, she confronts it head-on and sets the record straight. Throughout the years, I have seen Sean/a learn to trust and honor her unique path. She has fearlessly handled bigotry, hatred, and violence and has emerged with even more faith in the collective good.

Because of her nonapologetic approach, Sean/a has sometimes been cast away from various affiliations or groups. In response, and despite suffering much mental distress, Sean/a chose to create her own Category of One. Her example of withstanding adversity renews my confidence in the virtues driving our spiritual selves forward.

One primary objective of this book is to elucidate the deepest aspects of Sean/a's struggle in order that others may benefit and find healing on their own journeys. Sean/a and I have worked on her story together every step of the way so that her tale may be told with respect and compassion.

She has struggled through her search for self-acceptance while serving as a model of what true surviving and thriving can look like. In the face of judgment and bullying, harassment, and threats, she has attempted to keep her composure and simply move forward. I believe the manner in which Sean/a lives her life can serve as a lesson to us all.

While reading these pages, try living a day in Sean/a's shoes, facing the moment-to-moment struggle of managing severe internal mental distress. It's a wonder to me sometimes how this remarkable character can function, let alone flourish and radiate such joy.

I hold a heart full of gratitude to Sean/a for sharing ten wonderful years of deep friendship, and for allowing me to be a part of her odyssey toward belonging and of profound healing.

I have had the good fortune of witnessing Sean/a courageously and ambitiously inviting her communities along on her liberation journey. With deep respect and appreciation for the gems of wisdom she has brought forth from personal soul mining, I am thrilled at the opportunity to share refractions of those jewels with you by way of this book.

I hope reading her story will encourage you to openly consider those considered "different" in a spirit of teachability and wonder—to see the world from the colorful, wise perspective of someone who has learned to defy categories, embrace diversity, exude self-acceptance, and teach tolerance above all. In sharing Sean/a's story, I trust that, as a society, we will choose to move away from institutional betrayal of those who have been historically marginalized and relegated to the shadows. May we collectively take brave steps toward institutional change by having the courage to act with grace and acceptance.

It has been a journey in itself to find the right balance between "educational missive" and "exploratory memoir" while writing this book. I hope you can forgive the parts that digress a bit from the propelling action to give way for reflections and integrative understanding. In parallel process with Sean/a's life, we've made room for both.

For ease, Sean/a and I have decided the pronouns used for Sean/a will generally be she/her, unless describing a situation directly related to Sean. In the latter case, he/him will be used. Although Sean/a could be considered the quintessential "they," we have opted to tell her story from the singular perspective for minimal confusion.

Thank you, Coach, Teacher, Mentor, Friend. Thank you, Sean/a, for the many insights and life lessons you have illuminated during your journey! May this book be a beacon—shining the light in a new direction of compassion and acceptance—and a safe harbor—offering hope that there is a place of belonging for each of us as the unique, beautiful individuals that we are.

CHAPTER 1

Shelter for Sean/a

"Eight years. Sometimes I look at myself and say, 'Did I really go through this?' Homelessness is something no one should go through. To be abandoned or neglected is a terrible thing."

~Sean/a

What a wild downpour. Why was I out getting groceries that night? I can't remember. But there she was again.

Sean/a wore a yellow bikini top and a miniskirt, no jacket. She was clutching goose-bumped arms yet greeted me with a genuine smile as I approached the store, safe underneath my umbrella.

"Why aren't you home out of the cold?" I asked, pausing for a moment near the entrance.

She smiled and gave a hearty laugh. "Can't let a little weather stop me. I'm just *starting* my walk for the night."

"A *little* weather?" A roll of thunder punctuated my question. "Okay, well, stay safe!"

I hurried into the warmth of the store as she stepped into the storm, looking more like she was headed to a beach party than a drenching late-night excursion.

By then, I was starting to grow accustomed to Sean/a's eccentricities.

~ ~ ~

A few years earlier, my family and I had just moved to the gorgeous community of La Jolla, a coastal suburb of San Diego, with colorful flowers abundant in every neighborhood and its cosmopolitan yet chilled-out surfing vibe. It felt like the ideal place to raise a family. I loved connecting with people of all cultures and backgrounds every time I ran an errand or drove my daughter to soccer practice.

One of these people who we couldn't help but notice was Sean, a vibrant, gregarious member of the community who had been part of the La Jolla landscape for many years. Sean seemed to perfectly represent our new, friendly, somewhat-eccentric-yet-elegant hometown.

About a year later, sometime in 2015, my then-husband James and I noticed that Sean had switched from wearing sporty male clothing to women's athletic tops and tennis skirts, often in hot pink and other vibrant colors. She'd complete the look with a long, flowing wig. As a psychologist and humanitarian, I was instantly intrigued. I wanted to learn more about Sean/a's story.

One winter morning, I pulled into a community parking lot and noticed Sean/a sitting on a bench, shivering.

"Hey," I called out to her, "I have a couple of sweaters in the trunk that I was going to take to Goodwill. You can choose some for yourself."

Sean/a smiled broadly and followed me to the car. I popped open the trunk, letting her take a look at the giveaway items I had gathered. Also in my trunk was an old cashmere trench coat that had belonged to my father. I was planning to take it to the dry cleaners.

CHAPTER 1

She reached for the trench coat and lifted it out of its place. "Oh, wow," she said, placing it around her shoulders. "It's so warm. And look, it's actually long enough!" Sean/a elegantly pulled it on.

I smiled to myself. "It's yours," I told her. She browsed the trunk a little longer and chose a few pairs of Lululemon leggings that my daughter no longer wanted.

Only later did I find out that most of these items ended up at Goodwill after all, part of an endless rotation of Sean/a bringing in worn items in exchange for new, vibrant clothing. I suppose some lucky person in La Jolla has a debonair cashmere coat that used to belong to my British father.

A few weeks prior to running into Sean/a that stormy night, I noticed her hanging around the Starbucks inside of the Vons grocery nearby. I casually mentioned to the barista that I wanted to buy a drink for Sean/a as well.

"Oh, she's the kindest person," the barista said. "She has a most unusual story."

My curiosity increased. I tried to figure out how best to approach Sean/a without it being awkward or obvious. I clandestinely dropped a five-dollar bill and made a display of picking it up, as if finding it for the first time.

Looking over at Sean/a, I said, "You must have dropped this." She looked at me quizzically, then slowly took the bill. I asked if I could get her a Starbucks drink and she accepted. While waiting for her hot chocolate, we struck up a conversation.

"You have terrific style," I told her.

"Like Tina Turner?" she asked out of the blue.

I laughed. "Maybe. Yeah, why not?"

"Folks over at the La Jolla Music Society told me that Tina Turner could be my mom," Sean/a said. "I'm proud of the resemblance."

After our brief encounter, I searched for a magazine photo of Tina Turner on a whim and cut it out. I brought it with me the next time I visited Vons—the one place I was almost sure to see Sean/a.

"Your friends at the Music Society were right," I told her, offering Sean/a the magazine page.

"Oh my God." Sean/a didn't seem at all ashamed of her tears when she held the photo. "Thank you." Her heartfelt gratitude and profound emotion made me feel as if I had been given a glimpse of her soul.

Not long afterward was that night I spotted her outside Vons in the torrential rain. Sean/a usually spent hours there, chatting with customers, making the most of the warmth and comfort of the grocery store. But it was nearing closing time, and she had just been asked to leave.

I felt uneasy at the thought of her heading out into the storm. As she bounced around the corner starting her walk down Fay Street, I chased her down.

"Do you need shelter? A place to stay tonight?" The words came out almost before I thought them.

"Yes, ma'am," she said without hesitation. "I could really use a hot shower. I'm already chilly."

The reality of what I'd just offered hit me, but there was no turning back now. I walked with her to a nearby hotel. On that brief walk in the freezing rain, I discovered a few more pieces of this intriguing puzzle. Sean/a had no money, no credit cards, and most importantly, no home.

"Where are all your things?" I asked. I held my umbrella as high as I could to accommodate her tall form. She was almost six and a half feet tall.

"Shopping cart," she answered simply, like she wasn't used to divulging so much personal information. She muttered something beneath her breath that I couldn't make out. "At the gas station down the street," she added.

"Wait, where have you been staying?" I asked incredulously. In all my time spotting her around La Jolla and watching her graciously interact with the people around her, it had never occurred to me that Sean/a was homeless.

"For the last few years, I've been sleeping outside the La Jolla Recreation Center. I mean, usually." She laughed and stuck her hand out from under the umbrella, catching a few drops in her hand. "Sometimes, the weather isn't great."

I shivered as a gust of wind blew the rain almost sideways. The umbrella did little to protect either of us.

"'They let me sleep inside sometimes," she added. "You know that restaurant over there?"

"Yes." As she pointed, I noted I'd passed it many times without giving it a second thought, and yet it could be the most important place in the world to someone with no refuge.

"I was sneaking into the restroom at night to sleep. But the rains have been so heavy recently. They flooded the interior. And it's just been ... cold!"

As we neared the hotel, she told me of two particularly frigid nights. Shock ran through my system as I listened to her describe waking to find her fingers and toes stiff with the cold, her body shivering uncontrollably. She could have frozen to death, and I hadn't even known she was homeless.

I felt humbled, almost ashamed. She had suffered homelessness for years while I had never experienced housing insecurity. "We'll get you out of the cold into a comfortable bed," I told her.

Sean/a threw her hands up in the air and started crying. Clearly, they were tears of joy. "Thank you," she said, gesturing toward the heavens.

While checking her into the hotel for the night, I had to speak with the manager. I signed the paperwork with my identification, agreeing to all indemnities. I understood it was a usual practice; someone had to bear the responsibility in case a hotel patron chose to do something crazy like destroy the property or abscond with the room's contents.

I took a leap of faith that night.

And I have never looked back.

I made it back to my car in the Vons parking lot sometime around midnight. I sat in the driver's seat with the heater on, feeling its warmth, which I had always taken for granted, and began to cry. Sean/a had smiled at me with sincerity despite the freezing rain, and had not uttered a word of complaint. We'd interacted plenty, but not once had she divulged that she had no shelter from the cold.

My mind raced. What if I had not asked if she had a place to spend the night? The worst could have happened. I needed to find a way to get her off the streets, maybe even find her a place of permanent shelter. Could such a thing be possible?

Several weeks earlier, during one of our Vons interactions, Sean/a had pulled an article from her purse and showed it to me. A Bishop's High School student had written a beautiful piece about her. Sean/a proudly told me how impressed she was by this budding young author, Jesse, and her ability to capture the heart of the story.

The article had revealed ways that Sean/a made a positive impact in the community—quietly helping businesses with errands and favors. But the article didn't mention that Sean/a was chronically unhoused. Maybe it was her pride that caused her to keep quiet about it; understandably, none of us want pity. Or perhaps she had grown accustomed to her situation and was simply making the best of it privately.

As I drove home, wipers sweeping away sheets of rain from my windshield, I thought of an article I'd recently read in the *La Jolla*

Light, our local newspaper. It highlighted a GoFundMe fundraiser for a street cleaner. I had never heard of this novel crowdfunding platform, but my mind was racing, making connections. I also recalled an article about a psychiatrist who had befriended a local homeless man and helped him with neuroprocessing therapy.

These stories, along with Jesse's article, infused me with the impetus and courage to vouch for Sean/a. She deserved to live with dignity and in safety. Perhaps, if others in the community learned of her plight, together we might arrive at a solution to help her. That very night, I dialed the *La Jolla Light* and left a lengthy voicemail for the editor, imploring her to summon the power of the community on Sean/a's behalf.

The next morning, I went to the hotel to check on Sean/a, greeting the morning staff at the front desk and explaining why I was there.

"You're here for Sean/a?" the woman asked.

I hesitated, hoping nothing bad had happened. I had planned to add a couple of nights to her stay. Were they already going to ask her to leave?

"Yes, Sean/a Smith," I confirmed.

A smile crossed the woman's face. "She is the most pleasant guest I've seen in years." Her smile turned into a laugh. "Friendly. Loves making conversation, even with strangers. She was up early and joined a fitness class in the gym. She's been busy making friends with other travelers passing through."

The woman pointed me toward the dining room and I thanked her, feeling both shocked and relieved. I stopped in the doorway, having spotted Sean/a sitting at a table across from an older couple. The way they were talking and laughing together, anyone would think they had known each other for years. The sound of Sean/a's exuberant laughter carried across the room.

I was in awe at the power of Sean/a's joyful personality. One night of relief from homelessness, and she was already transmitting her joy and peace to those around her—transforming even this little hotel "community." Again, I was struck with the thought that something had to be done about her situation. She needed a place to call home, out of the elements.

Over the next few weeks, I spent a fair bit of time trying to arrange stays for Sean/a at different hotels and motels within walking distance, places for her to briefly recoup while I debated options for a more permanent solution. It wasn't cheap, and my then-husband and I had differing opinions about this added expense in our budget. As pressure built, the strain in my marriage grew.

I started selling my high-fashion boots and designer clothing at Buffalo Exchange to buy one more night of respite for Sean/a. I knew these hotel stays were merely a stopgap solution and felt like a failure each time she had to go back onto the streets. While Sean/a didn't complain, she confided in me one day that it was the worst feeling to go from safety and comfort to homelessness.

My desperation to help her find a lasting solution went up a thousand notches.

One morning shortly thereafter, I walked into a business meeting with my two Soul Wise Coaching (now Soul Wise Solutions) co-founders, Hilary and Cecile, and started crying as soon as the meeting started. I felt heavy with the burden of solving Sean/a's housing crisis on my own. Amidst tears, my story of the previous weeks' struggle came out. After hearing my distress, Hilary and Cecile immediately started tossing out ideas about how best to help Sean/a.

Part of our mission at Soul Wise was helping women in transition. We were accustomed to creating groups and offering help to women who were facing all sorts of changes—from dealing with teens and their struggles, to women facing extreme abuse or managing the chaos and uncertainty of menopause and aging. Seana fit the bill.

"We will do this together," Hilary assured me. With her marketing background, she promptly started researching how to set up a GoFundMe account. Cecile used her supportive, practical, business-oriented brain to generate a plan to fundraise on Sean/a's behalf, specifically to find her permanent shelter.

The editor from the local paper serendipitously called after returning from vacation and I immediately got to work on briefing them about Sean/a in an interview, feeling a sense of peace and resonance I hadn't felt in several weeks. I got a glimpse of what it means to belong to something greater than the three of us—creating a safety net for a woman in true transition. Our mission, Shelter for Shauna,[1] had begun. Hopefully, the strength of our trio would work toward fortifying her future.

We each took on tasks based on our areas of expertise. I contacted a dear artist friend, Robin, who agreed to do a drawing of Sean/a, as well as make bracelets for Sean/a to sell and give as a thank you to those who donated. Cecile offered her restaurant for a fundraiser in which Hilary performed uplifting tracks from her empowering CD, to rally the community in support of Sean/a.

I contacted Renee, an inspiring and influential friend who had spent twenty years in local media. She, in turn, contacted her local television crew to interview Sean/a and Soul Wise. The *San Diego Tribune* ran her story. Pat, an incredible humanitarian and the *La Jolla Light* reporter who wrote the ensuing Sean/a articles, told me the stories he wrote about Sean/a had also been published in the *Chicago Sun-Times*.

---

1 In later years, she would change the spelling "Shauna" to resemble her birth name, Sean, after Sean Connery, the original 007. It was apropos given the many adventures she has amassed in her life.

Momentum was building around this uniquely inspiring individual. The community, to whom Sean/a had dedicated her love one small act at a time, returned that love to her donation by donation.

All month as we ran our fundraising campaign, the phone buzzed as the people of La Jolla donated five, twenty, five hundred, and even one thousand dollars. Hilary had posted $10,000 as our goal—and the total eventually exceeded $11,000.

People showed up. They cared.

After the first donations rolled in, I contracted with a local hotel for Sean/a to stay for a month to six weeks while we dealt with the logistics involved in securing an apartment. It was no easy task considering her lack of rental and credit history.

While I was so grateful for the help being poured out by the community, some things grew more complicated by sharing Sean/a's story far and wide. It appeared that news of La Jollans helping Sean/a had sent a ripple effect through the San Diego homeless grapevine. Suddenly I was being contacted by people all over town who needed help.

In the process of navigating the obstacles to obtaining shelter, I was quickly schooled as to why the homeless crisis has reached epic proportions. We encountered one frustration after another trying to secure beds for people with housing insecurity, bringing them out of the elements and into safety. It is no wonder so many "prefer" to reside outside without restrictions and harassment.

Alarmingly, I also heard that some in the homeless community were harassing Sean/a on the city bus, quizzing her about how she got so fortunate and then bullying her, or mocking her in the lunch line of a local church that offered free sandwiches. She finally stopped going to that church, resorting back to the free breakfast, lunch, and dinner cycle she had with various restaurant managers she had done errands for around town. Peacefully, she awaited a homecooked burrito or pizza out the back door as a thank you before regular customers arrived or after they left.

~ ~ ~

One day, in the middle of all these changes, we met up at Starbucks in Vons. Sean/a and I found a small table.

"How are you doing?" I asked.

"So much has changed." She leaned forward, her hands wrapped around a steaming cup. "There were days that I got really tired of the cold walks and cold showers, but I knew the sun was going to shine."

"You've exchanged one type of challenge for some others," I observed. "Is it a relief or a burden?"

"You learn to adapt and accept," she told me, sitting back and taking a sip of her drink. "I don't think people really realize the experience of eight years outside."

"What kept you going through the darkest days?" I asked, eager for her response. I wanted to know what had given Sean/a strength to persevere with such an enthusiastic and positive demeanor despite her situation.

"Well, I didn't really think about it. Fact before emotion."

I was even more curious. Eight years is a long time to be unhoused and not really think much about it. "What do you mean by that?"

"I mean focusing on fact, on truth. You will only heal yourself if you tell the truth about yourself to yourself and others." She offered me that genuine smile I was growing accustomed to seeing. "It made me feel safe when kind people would say, 'You're okay.' I claimed that truth for myself. I just knew something was in store for me, that the suffering was going to end, that something was going to happen."

"That's powerful, Sean/a." The journey wasn't over and there were still plenty of challenges before us, but her perspective made me all the more certain that we were doing the right thing. It was going to be worth it.

"I'm not cynical, jaded, or angry," she added. "I try and stay positive. I think that saved me."

I nodded, thinking of how Sean/a actively invited curiosity from others and did not hesitate to offer a helping hand wherever she could. I thought about her practice of collecting glass bottles and other recyclables for various neighbors around town, which provided Sean/a with some income as she did the favor of clearing their terraces of trash. It was probably validating to receive those helping hands in return.

The money raised via GoFundMe was quickly being depleted—used to support all aspects of her life that had been neglected for so long. At one point I asked her if there was anything she had wanted the most in all her years without a home.

"Dental care," she told me with barely a moment's hesitation. Her response surprised me at first. Then it reminded me how I took these things for granted. Things I would consider the most basic needs had been her deepest desire.

As we tried to stay on top of sending out thank-you notes and special Sean/a bracelets to the donors while considering options for long-term housing, I couldn't neglect my responsibilities as a mother raising three children: my daughter who played competitive soccer with constant travel, and two stepdaughters, one with special needs.

Sometimes it was a lot to juggle, but whenever things began to feel like too much, something always happened to encourage me, letting me know that I was on the right track.

One evening, scanning my inbox, I opened an email from a couple, Lisa and David, who called themselves angel investors. Their Water-Walking Foundation gave one-time grants of up to fifteen thousand dollars to help people in great need who could positively impact their communities.

I immediately jumped on board, filling out an application for Sean/a. The interest of this remarkable couple didn't stop there, though. David surprised me by going all in on finding an apartment for Sean/a. He told me about connecting with a generous-hearted landlord named Lou who had read Sean/a's story and was supportive of her journey. Lou, also active in the LGBTQIA community, understood the discrimination and difficulties Sean/a continued to face.

As David sorted out the details of a one-year lease agreement with Lou, two other realtors from the LGBTQIA community contacted us. They were interested in helping Sean/a and joining forces with her regarding anti-bullying. Their support encouraged her to consider becoming an active voice with Project Bully-Buster.

As I had hoped, but had hardly dared to dream, the community was truly showing up for Sean/a—lending its strength while supporting and encouraging her desire to live boldly and beautifully in her truth, as she wished to show up in this world. Her positive and gregarious attitude motivated them, just as it had inspired me.

At the time, I had a rule that I wouldn't take Sean/a in my car (per my ex-husband's request regarding maintaining boundaries). I made all our plans for meetups taking into account how long it would take her to walk there.

One day, just after she got the keys to her apartment, Lisa called me. "Hey, David and I were planning to take Sean/a to Jerome's Furniture. We thought it would be a fun outing to decorate her apartment." It's hard to express the gratitude I felt at having others just as invested as I was in seeing Sean/a survive and thrive in her new living situation.

It was early evening when I got to her new place—a studio in La Jolla within walking distance of all the places Sean/a knew and frequented. Her exuberance was contagious as she showed me her new couch/futon/bed, her own artwork on the walls, and other furnishings in a clean, minimalist style.

"I can't believe my good fortune," she said time and again.

I noticed she had chosen all white for her surroundings.

"White is bright and happy. And I'm gonna keep everything beautiful," she exclaimed proudly.

From that time onward, I noticed a change beginning in Sean/a. Getting the keys to her apartment—her own safe space to let her guard down—gave Sean/a keys to other spaces, remote and deep places within herself. From there, she began opening herself more and more to trusting life's flow and following to see where it might lead her.

From the moment she gave herself that permission—to trust and live her life as she desired—Sean/a began telling her story more boldly. She would start chatting with young people in the Vons parking lot, wholeheartedly encouraging them to live their lives as they saw fit.

But her journey toward healing and wholeness, acceptance and belonging, had only just begun. New complications kept popping up all the time.

Thank You!

Because of you
Shauna has shelter.

With Gratitude,
Soulwise

Artist: Robin Wade

CHAPTER 2

A New Normal

"I still can't believe I lived at the rec center for four years and [was] homeless for eight. Now I have my own fridge, my own space. No more storing things all over town. I have an oven, a microwave. Now I have my own mattress, my own sheets and comforters and pillows, and at nighttime I can sleep!! How I look forward to sleep!"

~ Sean/a

It was a veritable whirlwind getting Sean/a settled. And it took a community. I was scurrying all over the nation for my daughter's soccer tournaments, so I set up a small bank account for Sean/a to manage her expenses in my absence. I quickly became aware that life on the streets hadn't taught her much about budgeting.

"I might need a little more to make it through the week," her latest note read.

I bit my lip, trying to figure out how to respond. While I didn't have a problem helping her make ends meet, I also knew that this money needed to stretch over a long-term basis.

When I got back home, I asked through the *La Jolla Light* if there was anyone with financial expertise who could help Sean/a manage her money, assist her in creating a budget, and teach her to make good financial decisions on her own.

A miracle worker, Sarah—who worked for a wealth management company—stepped up to the plate. She offered to take Sean/a grocery shopping and helped her learn to shop for and prepare nutritious meals on a budget.

Sarah didn't stop there. She also helped Sean/a create a resume. She was incredibly kind, respectful, knowledgeable, patient, and genuinely invested in Sean/a's progress. Sarah's tutelage had a terrific impact on Sean/a, whose input helped in a variety of areas—from buying bus cards to looking for the cheapest sale racks to paying her bills on time. It was a heartwarming example of humanity and community: a stranger reaching out to uplift another and pass on hard-won wisdom and skills.

Eventually, Sean/a became more proficient at meeting her own needs for sustenance. She was used to shopping for sale items and used goods at thrift stores. It amazed me how much she could find for a few dollars.

Since Sean/a had numerous friends at Wells Fargo inside Vons, it was natural for us to open her first account there and ever so slowly build her credit, starting with a secured bank card that had a $300 limit.

One of the goals of getting Sean/a housed was to create stability in her daily life by working up the hierarchy of needs, beginning with basic safety and security.[2] I found, however, that these needs would sometimes overlap and show themselves in interesting ways.

2 This refers to Maslow's hierarchy of needs, a psychological theory proposed by American psychologist Abraham Maslow, in which human needs are arranged in a hierarchical pyramid, with physiological needs such as food, shelter, and clothing providing the basis or foundation and self-actualization being at the apex.

For example, I discovered that Sean/a was hesitant to use the kitchen in her apartment; I couldn't figure out the reasoning for this. Was it the years she had spent homeless that explained this reluctance?

Thankfully, Sarah inspired Sean/a to use the microwave for cooking and taught her how to cook vegetables in a bag as well as use a blender to make healthy green juice. This one money-saving technique allowed Sean/a to avoid buying expensive green juices at the local juicer, although we still enjoyed meeting up at Juice Crafters for an occasional healthy treat.

Sean/a expressed willingness to learn and embrace many new skills as well as relearn old ones. It wasn't for lack of trying or hesitance to attempt something such as cleaning a bathroom. It was simply because she had been in sheer survival mode for such a long time (using public restrooms, etc.) that she forgot what it was like to truly and completely care for herself as well as for her surroundings.

Once she was housed in her La Jolla apartment, I had my housekeeper clean for her every three weeks just to make sure Sean/a's apartment was kept in good shape. It also made a difference in her level of self-acceptance that she was being cared for, understanding that she deserved the good things happening to her.

As we were ironing out the details of her move and giving television and newspaper interviews, I noticed a subtle transformation in both of us. We were really starting to believe that—by the sheer force of our belief in the goodness of people—the life Sean/a had envisioned could truly come to fruition. Her enthusiasm was contagious, and people were drawn in to help and play a part.

Where I had previously been scraping money together—through taking a car title loan, pawning my jewelry, selling my clothing—now others were pitching in. My parents and brother, extended family members, friends, and the community at large helped at various times to cover Sean/a's rent, electric bills, and cell phone payment. Some of them also sent money on a limited weekly basis to help with her grocery bills.

Sean/a started to acclimate to the structure and safety of her new life. It was an exciting, joyful time when everything was fresh and new. It awed her that she had her own mailbox, a key to her own place, and privacy—with complete control over her things and her time. Being off the streets and having the freedom to choose her own routine (rather than making choices out of necessity or safety considerations) were easy adjustments. Physical ones.

Harder, though, were the mental adjustments to her newfound situation. Some old habits were hard to break.

On my return from a soccer trip, I met an acquaintance while out in town. She greeted me and asked how Sean/a was doing, then added, "I thought she had a place to stay."

"She does," I assured the woman.

The woman nodded slowly, as if deciding how much she wanted to say.

"What is it?" I asked.

She avoided my inquisitive glance. "Well, I saw her outside the Verizon store the other day, just sitting there. I was on my way to run some errands, and on my way back in the afternoon, she was still hanging out there, like she used to, you know?"

It took me some time to understand that the mere acts of lounging at home watching television, cleaning, or surfing the web on her newly donated laptop were completely foreign to Sean/a. Her "television screen" had always consisted of passersby and the living, breathing, external world.

While she slowly adjusted to her new and much improved normal, the whirlwind of getting Sean/a settled required all hands on deck. She faced a myriad of challenges in these efforts to rebuild her life. For instance, while homeless, she had fallen through the cracks of social services, and it took time to gather needed documents and legal papers to obtain the help she needed.

After so many years unhoused with no identification, she cherished every document that we painstakingly obtained for her. Sean/a framed and laminated some and was careful to tuck a few copies into her purse on the off chance she might be stopped on the street for questioning. (My impression is that this happened to her quite a bit during her years unhoused and left a traumatic imprint.) The harassment and justifications that ensued must have been insufferable for her.

As she slowly rebuilt her life, we followed up on every lead that offered assistance. Sean/a enthusiastically did her part by walking all over the community to pick up donated items. Generous La Jollans offered kitchen supplies, bedding, clothing, and much more. Brian and Arielle, who had been quietly restoring humanity and dignity to the homeless for years, were two such compassionate souls who responded to the articles we posted about Sean/a in *La Jolla Light*. Sean/a was overjoyed to carry the baskets of silk pillowcases and towels they had collected for her; she felt like the Queen of La Jolla.

Sean/a's crisis being made known brought forth the healers and givers that the community was proud to call its own. So many rallied behind her as allies and social support. They helped her find self-sustaining endeavors and projects as she not only transitioned from homeless to housed, but also from living as Sean to Sean/a.

It truly took a village—California's jewel.

~ ~ ~

Once she was able to trust her new living arrangement, Sean/a's conversations became more revelatory of the post-traumatic stress she'd been dealing with for years. In our Juice Crafters meetups for an acai bowl, I slowly came to understand the salient features of her transition from Sean to Sean/a and from homeless to housed.

Life on the streets had evoked a survival instinct that guided her to befriend and connect with others. This wasn't easy, however, as she rarely knew who she could depend on for help. Sean/a balanced a hopeful yet restless energy behind every movement. While un-housed, she felt the need to keep moving, lest her temporary bath-room shelter vanish or the gas station manager (who let her store her things out back during the day) change his mind.

As she became bolder in her new identity, Sean/a revealed more daring levels of herself, showing vulnerability deep beneath the surface. She grew, in time, to attribute her difficulty controlling occasional outbursts—which sometimes startled passersby—as a complex post-traumatic stress reaction to so many years living on the streets. She also began to name the daily confusion she had felt about adjusting to and more fully integrating her intersex condition (explored in a later chapter).

I wanted to understand the extent of Sean/a's mental struggles, yet these matters were hard for her to articulate. As a board-certified expert on Traumatic Stress, I knew there was much more to the story. I sensed that a biologically driven brain chemistry imbalance had something to do with her current state. At the same time, I believed that the same biochemistry that gave rise to delusions and psychoses was also a funda-mental source of her extreme optimism and survival strengths.

But there was no way to tease apart which aspects of her char-acter and demeanor were physiological, which were psychological, and what parts had been deeply affected by her past. I had no desire to pass judgment upon the life-saving defenses of her mind and spirit. These parts of her personality that some might have considered odd or off-putting were those very things in which she had found strength and the ability to endure through years of homelessness and uncertainty.

Over time, I witnessed the emergence of a more grounded, calmer Sean/a. She finally had the opportunity to develop her personality away from the cultural influences that had been projected upon her daily while she was homeless. The corner where Sean/a had spent so much time sitting was the theater in which she'd lived a highly public life. Everywhere she went, she had to deal with a relentless invasion of privacy and public scrutiny, without a break.

As an unhoused individual, she'd had no other recourse. Now, with a place of her own, she was learning the power of choice. It took time—emotionally and practically—but Sean/a outgrew that street corner. She found freedom in being able to choose when, where, and how she wished to be seen.

Interestingly, I heard from folks in the community who missed passing Sean/a in her reliable spot on the corner. Some of them asked why I had intervened to get her off the streets; they had grown to love seeing her energy and creativity. But this way of being had placed Sean/a as the object for another's interest or amusement. True consideration of Sean/a's needs hadn't necessarily been a factor.

I believe that what drew me and others toward Sean/a was her joie de vivre. She had a wonderful gift of connection and community-building … with anyone and everyone. Everybody in the La Jolla community knew Sean/a.

Rather than coming across as disenfranchised, she was engaged in other people's lives and appeared content amidst the daily struggles she obviously endured. One would not have known Sean/a was homeless or that she struggled from mental distress unless a person paid keen attention to her daily routine. This was one of the reasons it took me so long to realize she was unhoused.

Because of her endless rotation of colorful Goodwill outfits, as well as her good hygiene and positive attitude, I had been unaware (like many in the community) that Sean/a was living on the streets, much less that she was in an existential struggle to understand herself and her place in the world. In spite of deep introspections and meta-concerns, her positivity and a well of inner strength propelled her forward.

I slowly grew to grasp the complexity of Sean/a's responses to her years of trauma, homelessness, and struggles with identity. The toll these experiences exacted on her will likely never be completely understood. I found it extraordinary—the way she had struggled so deeply with identity and suffered offenses against her dignity, yet she continued to express valiance, trust, and courage in building her life back up from ground zero.

In my work as a psychologist studying and treating trauma disorders, I've seen time and again how the traumata the most vulnerable members of our population endure—both as children and adults—are skewed and forged into whatever is convenient for the abuser or those in power holding the dominant narrative. This often forces those in marginalized spaces—including the abused and people suffering from mental illness—to deny their own reality.

The toxic effect this has is multiplied a thousandfold when their offenders cultivate outward images that are in line with society's purported ideals. As a result, the socially constructed illusions are validated while the truth of the trauma survivor is repeatedly silenced.

In Sean/a's case, it took her a while to embrace the normalcy of life without the struggles that being unhoused for so long had presented. It has not been an easy road, this ubiquitous search for belonging. And the journey continued.

Artist: Robin Wade

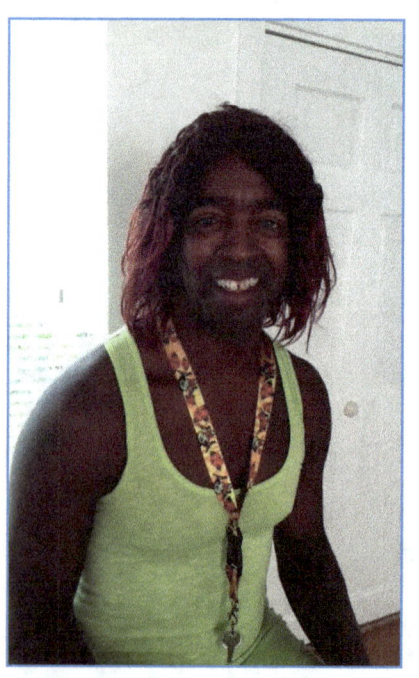
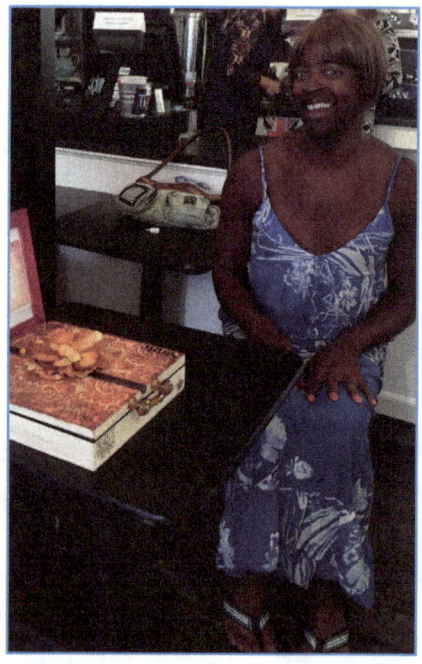

Group works to find 'Shelter for Shauna'

■ Initiative to help women in transition
begins with homeless, La Jolla individual

BY PAT SHERMAN

Wise Coaching co-founders Cecile Ward, Kirsten Harrison-Jack and Hilary Michels
...ng are launching 'Shelter for Shauna' fundraising initiative and hope to create
...r initiatives to help women facing extreme life challenges. PHOTOS BY PAT SHERMAN

●●○○○ Verizon   LTE   **12:08 AM**   ☾ ⊀ **85%** ▬

lajollalight.com

 LA JOLLA LIGHT

Shauna off streets and settled in new apartment

By Pat Sherman 02:47p.m. Jun 23, 2015

Shauna Smith moved into this studio apartment in the

Village, June 22. Rent and utilities have been prepaid for

one year while she works to get her life back on track. —

Pat Sherman

Angel investors step forward to help

Photo taken in 2025, with Sean/a pointing out where she slept on cardboard for four years.

CHAPTER 3

Backstory

"In the early years, I knew something was going on inside, I knew something wasn't coming together. It made sense, but only so far. There were moments when it just got to be a little too much. I thought they were hiding me at the rec center because they knew something about me was different."

~ Sean/a

One day after work, I saw a voicemail message from Lou, Sean/a's landlord, asking me to call him as soon as possible. Worried that something might have happened to Sean/a, I dialed him back right away.

"Kirsten," he said, answering on the second ring, "I got a call from a woman who claims to be Sean/a's sister."

It took me a few seconds to absorb what Lou was saying. Sean/a never talked about her family. "Sean/a's sister?" I echoed.

"Yep, I'm not really sure what to make of it. She told me she looked up my contact info after seeing the *La Jolla Light* article that mentioned I rented an apartment to Sean/a."

I knew the article he was talking about. It had mentioned Lou and expressed gratitude for his generosity. Was someone trying to scam him … or Sean/a?

"Anyway," he continued, "I'm not sure of the veracity of her claim, so figured I'd better call you up."

"Thanks, Lou," I answered, not sure myself what to make of it. "What did you tell the woman?"

"Well, I didn't give her any personal information. It's important to protect the privacy of my tenants. But the woman—her name is Robin—gave me her number, said she'd love to be back in touch with … well, she used the name Sean."

I took down the number and thanked Lou. After the call, I tried to sort it out in my mind. Was it some kind of scam? Or was this lady legit?

Only one way to find out. My hands felt a little shaky as I dialed the phone number Lou gave me. I didn't know what to expect. A woman answered.

"Hi," I said, feeling hesitant and not knowing where to start. "I got your contact information from Lou."

"Oh, is this about Sean?" she asked right away. I could sense a blend of excitement and anxiety in her voice.

"Yes. May I ask who I'm speaking to?" I wanted to make sure this was the same person who'd phoned Lou.

"I'm Robin, Sean's sister."

I took a deep breath and introduced myself, explaining my connection to Sean/a.

"I can't believe it. I thought he had …" Robin's voice broke. "It's been over a decade since I heard from Sean. I didn't know if he was even alive." I heard her softly crying at the other end of the line.

44

CHAPTER 3

We spoke for nearly two hours. She explained that her daughter had decided, on a whim, to look up Sean Smith in San Diego. The *La Jolla Light* article and Shelter for Shauna GoFundMe had been published a few months prior. Robin's daughter had not only found her uncle but discovered her uncle was now her aunt.

"She showed me a photo of Sean … uh, Sean/a. I … I was speechless," Robin said. "My brother was present at my daughter's birth, you know?"

As we talked, it became clear to me that Robin was ready to jump on a plane right then and there to visit Sean/a. It was like a ghost had come back, but no longer a ghost—her long-lost family member, resurrected.

I assured her I would speak to Sean/a and pass on her eagerness to reconnect.

The next day, I met up with Sean/a and eagerly launched into the details of my conversation with Robin. So absorbed was I in my excitement that I didn't notice her response was hesitant, trepidatious.

"Seriously, she's ready to get on a flight and come see you." I finally paused. "What do you think?"

"Wow, Doc." She leaned forward and put her head in her hands for a minute.

"Sean/a, are you okay?"

Sean/a sat up straight again and looked at me. "It's like, my whole life just flashed before me, all the pain of living homeless. They were hard times, but I just couldn't tell my family I didn't have a place to go. No matter how hard it was."

I sat in silence, waiting for her to process this news. Perhaps I should have eased into the conversation. Clearly, it was a lot for Sean/a to take in.

After a moment, a huge smile graced her face. "But I really have two grandnephews?"

I smiled back. "Yes, that's what Robin said."

She shook her head. "It's ... overwhelming."

I didn't want to push for anything. Sean/a was newly housed, her story only recently having gone public via the fundraiser and articles. It was a strange paradox. Although she had previously been in the public eye in a manner of speaking, due to her homelessness, she had been living a life of relative obscurity. Now, although she had four walls surrounding her, in another way she was dealing with a complete lack of privacy due to word about her life and situation going somewhat viral.

Understandably, this brought about feelings of vulnerability. And now her family had gotten in touch after years of no contact. Sean/a wasn't ready for a full-on reunion.

She did, however, consent to a visit from her niece, Annya—the one who had searched online and found news about Sean/a. In the days leading up to the mini-reunion, Sean/a oscillated between feeling overjoyed and nervous.

One beautiful afternoon, Annya flew into town and met Sean/a at the local Juice Caboose for a smoothie and a catch-up.

"She's grown into a brilliant woman," Sean/a told me after the meeting, "and absolutely loved that she was able to be the family liaison, bringing tidings from her mom."

"But you're not quite ready to meet up with Robin?" I asked.

"No, not yet," Sean/a said. "I hope she'll understand. I love my family. It's just ..." Her words trailed off.

"I think she'll understand," I said, reflecting on my phone conversation with Robin.

"My sister is a special person. I haven't seen her in so long, though, you know? The last time I saw her was in 2000, I think."

"I'm pretty sure she's just happy to know you're doing okay ... that you're alive and safe."

Sean/a laughed. "Yeah, that's Robin for sure. I remember she was always taking care of me, and Ann would say, 'Don't get Sean into trouble.' I always tried to listen to her. She was helpful to me in so many ways."

"Ann?" I queried.

"My mother. She was a sweet lady, and so beautiful," Sean/a recollected. "She left this earth way too soon; I think she was just 49."

"I'm sorry."

Sean/a shook her head. "No, it's alright, Doc. Remember? Tina Turner is my mother, in my soul."

I laughed and shook my head. "Right, I'd forgotten."

"Family history is important. If you haven't learned who your mother and father really are, you can be very confused growing up." Her statement felt like it was coming out of the blue. "Welcome to my world," she added.

I waited for her to say more about that "world," but she didn't.

"That reminds me," I said. "Robin asked if you'd be okay with my giving you her number. In case you wanted to reach out. She promised she's not going to show up at your door or anything."

"I think that would be fine." Sean/a nodded. "It was pretty great to spend time with Annya. It's overwhelming how quickly kids grow up."

I also had the privilege of speaking with Sean/a's nephew, Joshua. We talked at length about what he had heard about Sean/a and who he remembered Sean to be. Joshua was very considerate of his mother's wish to reunite with her only living sibling.

Sean/a's family was gracious and loving. While I hoped for a sibling embrace after all these years, I decided to be the happy go-between—via calls and Facebook messages—for Sean/a and her family. Overall, Sean/a expressed gratitude at the opportunity to reconnect with her family in this way.

Out of respect for Sean/a's wish to be the one to reinitiate contact, Robin never called despite eventually also having Sean/a's phone number, yet she found ways to do special things for Sean/a.

For example, I treated Sean/a to a Valentine's spa weekend at a hotel in Carlsbad, about a half hour's drive away. It was the first time Sean/a had been out of La Jolla (and in a pool and hot tub) for many, many years. She relished wearing a bikini for the first time in her life. And of course, made a splash with the hotel staff and guests!

Robin sent her chocolate-covered strawberries through the hotel to top off that spa weekend. I was brought to tears by the beautiful gesture. Robin respected Sean/a's wishes and kept her distance, but she still honored the deep love of family between them.

When I again encouraged an in-person reconciliation or reunion, Sean/a said, "We probably do better each living our own lives, but I wish them well. I love my family."

Family can be bittersweet. For some, those foundational years can be sources of great joy and great pain. In receiving gestures such as those chocolate-covered strawberries from her sister, I believe Sean/a felt cherished, seen, and respected.

～～～

Sean/a was born in Los Angeles, California, as Sean Smith. At some point in very early childhood, Sean's family moved east to be near his dad's extended family in Washington, DC, and Baltimore, Maryland. After his parents' divorce, his mother remarried Jesse and they moved to Columbia, Maryland. Sean's family then moved to Colorado when he was 10 years old. In his senior year, the family moved again to Las Vegas, to be closer to his sister Robin, and this was where Sean graduated from high school.

By Seana's account, Sean felt his mother and sister were very close. She credits Robin for taking good care of Sean as a child. She told me, "Robin helped me out a lot when I was young, and I was there when my niece and nephews were born." In hearing her speak about Robin, I concluded that part of her reluctance at reuniting directly with her sister was fear regarding the deep emotionality of a reunion.

From Sean/a's perspective, her sister was often busy with extended relationships, so Sean felt like a fixture in his much older sister's life, attending weddings and the birth of her kids. As with many of us, they were both doing their very best to keep swimming upstream in search of better situations.

She reflected that Sean often just "went along for the ride" as a child, never quite knowing what was going to happen next or where he was going. He often felt lost in the shuffle. Every child has an innate need for an environment of stability, security, and control, and we all struggle in different ways when we fail to find that stable and secure foundation. School and speech therapy (due to a severe stutter) provided necessary structure, for a while at least.

When Robin moved away, Sean finally received the one-on-one attention he craved. The Black church and family were everything at the time, but some aspects of childhood were confusing, not least of which the fact that he was sometimes called Little Hermie (short for hermaphrodite) by mean-spirited classmates.

At the same time, Sean lived a sheltered life in many respects. Sean's older brother Mike was the first gay person he knew, but Sean was never told in concrete language that his brother was gay; he merely noticed Mike was extremely flamboyant in dress and manner.

"I didn't even know my brother was gay," Sean/a told me once. "In my extremely religious upbringing, the truth about my brother's homosexuality was hidden from me." She felt she had been kept out of the loop when it came to details about her older brother's life.

When Mike died of AIDS in the 1980s, Sean wasn't informed about his passing until a month after his death. And even then, the story was that he died of cancer. No one had those important conversations with her about gender and sexuality despite a slowly growing confusion that Sean never felt free to talk about. All she remembers was coming home from college on a break and Mike was no longer around. Sean had no idea of the private world or the private struggles in which his brother had lived and lived through.

To this day, Sean/a remembers her brother as the kindest man, saying, "He would give you the shirt off of his back." Robin concurs with this recollection.

~ ~ ~

In my role as a "liaison" of sorts between Sean/a and her sister—sending texts, photos, and videos at different junctures and holidays—I received a message from Robin that their stepfather, Jesse, had passed away.

Several times over the previous months, Sean/a had expressed to me what an honorable and kind man their stepfather was. With trepidation, I shared the sad news with her.

After the initial shock, she said, "I don't think I could go to a funeral. I would be so emotional, I wouldn't be able to handle it."

"It's okay, Sean/a. You don't need to feel obliged to go."

"There's no way I can express what this loss means," she added, "but I'd like to send a bouquet."

"We can do that," I assured her.

"Jesse was a good man. A really good man. It wasn't until Ann married him that I learned so much about being a good person with integrity and deep faith and values."

"I'm glad you have fond memories of him," I told her, thinking about the strong relationship I am blessed to have with my own father.

In the wake of this loss, Sean/a revealed more of her background. In her stories, she never wavered in her esteem for her stepfather, a devout pastor and family man who provided stability and a strong religious foundation for their family.

Jesse's influence served as a bedrock of support in Sean's life. She told me Jesse had even met with Barack Obama on one occasion, long before Obama became our nation's first Black president. It gave her great solace to send a message to her stepfather's congregation via her sister, Robin, expressing her condolences at his passing.

"Jesse's encouragement eventually directed me to attend Christian Heritage College," she reflected. "That decision was one of those that changed my life."

"Did you attend immediately after high school?" I asked, trying to get her journey straight in my mind.

"No, after high school, I attended Casper College on a basketball scholarship."

"In Wyoming?" I asked.

"You're telling me." Sean/a laughed as she reflected on the culture shock of moving to a small, predominantly white town in the mountains. It was a place she grew to love, a place where her coaches and teammates sustained her.

"I moved so much as a young person that I learned not to get too attached to anyone," she told me. "That U-Haul truck can be pretty powerful, a symbol for keeping on the move."

"But look at all the people skills you gained," I pointed out. "You're a master at reinventing yourself and thriving."

"I had to learn to adapt fast and I made friends easily," she agreed. "In high school I even made the prom king ballot, but I lost. I was very active in high school." From class treasurer to president, Sean had a knack for rallying communities together.

She eventually relocated to California and attended Christian Heritage College in El Cajon. Sean then followed a respected coach to San Diego and taught at Torrey Pines High School as a substitute teacher and assistant coach.

"When I first arrived in San Diego, my high school coach lived here and I thought the weather was amazing, the city was beautiful, and the people were nice." She loved the ability to drive from the malls to the beautiful beaches. "It was a far cry from shoveling snow and all the winter clothing and boots I had to wear in Wyoming."

"San Diego is beautiful," I agreed.

"And in the '80s it was three dollars a credit to go to community college. Can you believe it? I could go to school for nine dollars a course." Sean earned a four-year degree in PE; however, in the ensuing years while trying to build a career and a life, things began to unravel.

Ann

Jesse (center)

SR SEAN SMITH
UNITED STATES NAVY

USN VETERAN

FINAL RANK
Seaman Recruit

SERVICE YEARS
1988 - 1988

LAST NEC
SR-0000-Seaman Recruit

PRIMARY UNIT
1988-1988, Naval Base San Diego, CA

---

www.lajollalight.com

LA JOLLA LIGHT · SEPTEMBER 6, 2018 · PAGE **A15**

LA JOLLA NEWS NUGGETS (CONTINUED)

"I looked at what's known about pulsed RF/MW in relation to diplomats' experiences," said Golomb. "Everything fits. The specifics of the varied sounds that the diplomats reported hearing during the apparent inciting episodes, such as chirping, ringing and buzzing, cohere in detail with known properties of so-called 'microwave hearing.'"

Beginning in 2016, personnel at the U.S. Embassy in Havana, Cuba (as well as Canadian diplomats and family members) described hearing strange sounds, followed by an array of symptoms. Though some officials and media have described the events as "sonic attacks," some experts on sound have rejected this explanation. In May of this year, the State Department reported that U.S. government employees in Guangzhou, China had also experienced similar sounds and health problems.

Golomb's conclusions may aid in the treatment of the diplomats (and affected family members) and assist U.S.

government agencies seeking to determine the precise cause.

Shauna's moved on ...

The streets of La Jolla no longer have Shauna Smith roaming them. The polarizing 30-year La Jolla resident — whom locals tended to adore or abhor — has moved hundreds of miles away, to a desert community where, says longtime benefactor Kirsten Harrison-Jack, "she feels less judged and more at peace."

"She writes me a bazillion texts saying how much fun she's having," says Harrison-Jack, a La Jolla clinical psychologist who continues to cover Smith's rent and phone bills. "Nobody's judging her based on being different or sticking out."

After her year lease is up, Harrison-Jack says, Smith may stay where she is, move somewhere else or return to La Jolla.

According to Harrison-Jack, one of the

reasons Smith was always on La Jolla's streets — even after she was housed — was that her apartment in La Jolla was so tiny. "Now, she's got a normal-size one-bedroom," Harrison-Jack says. "It'll let her relax more and give her the peace and quiet she needs to get going on the book."

Smith and Harrison-Jack plan to collaborate on Smith's autobiography, as has been reported by the *Light* several times over the past three years.

"She's lived her life in so many marginalized categories — intersex, homeless, African-American — it's amazing that she has the inner strength, but she does," Harrison-Jack says.

Though she is Smith's benefactor, friend and co-author, Harrison-Jack wants it known that she has never served as her therapist or doctor. "It was raining really hard one night and I saw Shauna outside and I couldn't take it," she says. "I helped her get a hotel room and it progressed."

COURTESY

Clinical psychologist Kirsten Harrison-Jack and her friend, Shauna Smith, pose for a selfie prior to Smith's departure from La Jolla

---

BERKSHIRE HATHAWAY | California Properties
HomeServices

CHAPTER 4

A Rapid Descent

"My life was always work, work, work, and more work until—like a car running out of fuel—I just came to a halt. So, I started to eliminate one thing after the other. At one point, out of sheer exhaustion, I let things pile up. I got evicted and started living in my car. And then when the car was towed, I became homeless."

~ Sean/a

"It was during those years that I first thought something was off," she told me. "In my junior year of college, I had a chance to see a psychologist for a problem that my friend Trevor thought I might have."

It seems that Trevor recognized Sean was having difficulties understanding his identity and so directed him toward therapy. He also took Sean to the local mental health center.

"He was so smart; Trevor went to Yale Law School. I'll always be grateful to him for his help and care. I wish I had known about intersex back then."

"When did you learn about intersex?" I asked.

"I was fairly sheltered, you know. Remember, I didn't even know about my brother being gay. A dentist was the first person to refer me to a book about being gay and how to integrate that with Christianity."

"A dentist?" I echoed.

"Yeah, but the book totally opened my eyes to that idea that gay was not taboo, as I had been taught to believe."

Reading that book, the title of which Sean/a couldn't recall, was illuminating and forged a broader identity for Sean going forward. He enlisted in the US Navy in Las Vegas in 1988. He later received an honorable discharge for what he thought was a heart murmur but eventually realized had more to do with ambiguous genitalia and the intersex condition that had been a source of confusion for some time.

Sean moved back to San Diego in 1992, from Las Vegas. California became home once more. Sean loved that the people of California seemed to have such free spirits, how they were open and willing to take chances on being friends with new people. The fact that California offered the sense that a person could be whoever they wanted to be meant a lot to him even during these years when he was manifesting as Sean—the personality he had known all his life.

Sean/a remarked to me, "The first time I saw La Jolla, I fell in love with it. It seemed attainable. It was so special and wonderful; I knew I could live there." She was also touched by the passion for friendship and community, referring to it as "almost an art form."

"What were your goals in life during that time?" I asked her.

"Peace of mind," she responded. "I wanted answers to the questions 'Who am I?' and 'Where am I going?' I've never been entitled, but somehow, I just knew La Jolla was the place for me. It was quiet, secluded, and calming in its beauty." In part because of the ambiguity he felt about who he was, Sean appreciated the forward-thinking, intelligent residents who appeared more embracing of such uncertainty.

Sean began coaching. His first coaching job eventually led to him working 70 hours a week at the Boys and Girls Club. As she related it to me, the folks at the club loved Sean's enthusiasm but were also increasingly concerned by the number of hours he worked. "They thought I was having a bit of a manic unraveling and described me as always charged up," she said.

Sean was overspending credit limits at the time. As she related, "When I was in my fourth year of teaching and my bills were piling up, I had a lot of student loans. I started a payment plan, but it felt insurmountable. And it was."

He taught aerobics and did personal training on the side, as a personal basketball instructor all over San Diego County. Unfortunately, it wasn't enough to cover expenses. "I then filed for bankruptcy, and the only thing left was a car payment."

Although Sean had an apartment and car in Claremont, a ten-minute drive from La Jolla, he spent much of his time in this community. He loved the people in La Jolla because of how welcoming everyone was. Every afternoon after work, he used to go to the La Jolla Rec Center to play basketball, make friends, and enjoy the leisure social activity.

It was a very busy season. As she explained it to me, "I was still working seven days a week as a substitute and then at the Boys and Girls Club, and I ran a basketball league and a sports ministry. I was also doing personal training. But my bodily changes were catching up to me, mentally and physically, and I stopped teaching."

"Then I put the car payment on a credit card and my friend stepped in to help." Sean's sister and a friend both attempted to help pay the bills, but Sean was still unable to keep up. "I couldn't manage rent, food, gas, and insurance."

Sean started to eliminate one thing after another, out of sheer exhaustion. Expenses and bills quickly piled up and he was evicted from his apartment for back rent. That was when he started living in his car.

He still made valiant attempts to maintain his dignity. He would collect cans at the beach for gas and food money. Every day he took a shower and brushed his teeth at the public beach facilities, practicing good hygiene and grooming. Sean took full advantage of all public resources.

Then his car was towed, which marked an official descent into homelessness. That first night on the streets without any shelter, Sean thought to himself, *Well, I guess this is home now.* But it was scary. Very scary.

In addition to the general stress of living on the streets, one injustice after another was committed against Sean/a and her identity—which was in flux during these years—although she has always remained hesitant to relate the details of this confusing time.

I believe the adaptive aspects of Sean/a's mental challenges (and an apparent lack of insight into their origins) are in part what allowed her to remain calm in the face of extreme uncertainty. This is a unique gift I have sometimes encountered in my years studying PTSD and treating those with trauma disorders. A sense of an almost otherworldly guidance. Her remarkable sense of destiny and purpose has given her hope and an appreciation for life despite the challenges.

This heightened sense of omnipotence, to some, signals the grandiosity of mania or schizophrenia; however, I am not out to make a definitive diagnosis. Hers appears a complex admixture of biology, psychosocial stressors, and spiritual coping. My goal, rather, is to reliably share Sean/a's story.

In those early days of homelessness, she stayed with friends from time to time. Later, the manager of the La Jolla Rec Center allowed her to spend the night in a protected alcove outside the facility, with permission to use the center's kitchen and restrooms. She ended up staying there for four years. They took good care of her, even allowing her to teach basketball. However, a change in management left her adrift.

Thankfully, Sean/a's strong network and the sense of community she created all over La Jolla were the reason she never completely fell through the cracks. Regardless of mounting internal struggles, Sean/a still garnered the respect of those around her.

Hunger was a sensation she didn't feel often due to her resourcefulness and "people skills." One relationship at a time kept her cared for and fed. The manager at a Taco Bell in Pacific Beach gave her burritos every day for years. A neighborhood fish shop gave her clam chowder nightly for a year, which she credits with keeping her warm and nourishing her spirit.

She would run errands for the local taco shop, Rigoberto's. In exchange for food, she would go to the bank when they needed coins as well as pick up coffee for them. She recalled, "Sometimes the manager paid me five dollars to wash her car. The best thing she did for me was to trust me; I strived to always earn that trust and never let her down."

The Bruegger's bagel shop gave Sean/a their remaining bagels at 4:00 p.m. every day when they were closing. Whenever the rec center had senior dances, she would have dinner with them. The folks at the rec center also gave Sean/a Starbucks cards that lasted a whole summer. The local Jack in the Box made copies in their office for her.

The folks at the La Jolla Tennis Club encouraged her in many ways while she was struggling. Sean/a recalled, "They fed and clothed me. Whenever they had tournaments, they invited me to eat with them. The members gave me their old clothing and tennis shoes. One member even bought me a bike."

Reflectively, she summarized, "Can you believe the generosity of the community? Everyone has such busy lives and had worked so hard to get there and yet they still stopped to help me. One couple routinely gave me a twenty-dollar bill here and there, and the guys from Lamborghini gave me two hundred dollars once. Imagine that. I thought I went to heaven!"

While her friendliness and giving spirit enabled her to survive those times, I don't want to minimize the fact that Sean/a was homeless for eight years. She slept outside in the harsh elements on most occasions.

At times, it surprised me how Sean/a often seemed oblivious to physical sensations that most of us would register as uncomfortable, such as shivering in extreme cold but failing to put on warmer clothing or wearing shoes five sizes too small. I recognized, however, that there is adaptive value to such somatic dissociation if one is homeless. By detaching oneself from a situation of physical discomfort, for instance, one can focus primarily on survival needs.

As angel investors David and Lisa helped Sean/a furnish her apartment, Sean/a insisted on a reclining couch instead of a bed with a mattress. She slept on this comparatively hard surface for a while until I suggested we purchase a Casper mattress for her. After that, she raved about her "heavenly sleep" almost every time we got together. She walked with less pain in her hips and her back appeared straighter.

Sean/a wasn't even aware of the physical toll homelessness had wrought. As Sean/a grew more comfortable speaking about surviving years without a shelter to call her own, the somatic elements of her traumata seemed to visibly effuse from her viscera.

The restitutive and healing function of attending to her basic survival needs opened her entire being to the idea that *she deserved to take up space*, that she could *claim this space as her own*, and that she could comfortably stretch out and relax into that space. This empowered version of Sean/a wasn't filled with despair over lost years; rather, she was filled with gratitude and more determination to spread joy and hope.

However, it isn't as simple as that. The degree of decompensation[3] and regression Sean/a experienced when under severe duress—making her appear distressed and chaotic—is commensurate with accounts of what might have been early psychotic breaks she experienced in college, which likely continued through to her Navy discharge and beyond. Sean/a recognizes the combined factors of her changing body (and confusion therein), compounded with lack of sleep from an overstretched schedule and complex PTSD as all playing a part.

It's a classic "chicken or egg" phenomenon. Was she decompensating, and the stress of these times put her over the edge? Or was she stressed, which then caused her to unravel? The result was the same but—to Sean/a—its origin is important. It is difficult to tease apart the etiology of Sean/a's mystical, spiritual connection, her dissociative and depersonalized episodes, and what some would call her delusions of grandeur.

Some researchers in psychology have posited that transpersonal reality becomes available when one's consciousness is freed from its dependence on the physical body. Authors compare the out-of-body

3 As a psychiatric term, decompensation refers to the inability to demonstrate effective coping mechanisms when responding to stress, thus resulting in personality disturbances or disintegration, which can lead to schizophrenic episodes or relapses.

experience in nonlocal consciousness to schizophrenia, concluding that bodily distortions and identity issues vary greatly on opposite ends of a consciousness spectrum. In this respect, factors such as physical and mental health, mental distress, and transcendence serve as focal points orienting Sean/a at any given moment to her reality.

I witnessed Sean/a practicing humility, patience, and under-standing throughout a variety of challenges that didn't stop once she was safely housed. Her extensive mental distress from life on the streets and the stress and confusion of her earlier years, coupled with her biology, made her an ideal candidate for medical mental health intervention, but I could probably write a separate book on the difficulty of advocating for a formerly unhoused individual!

For instance, obtaining a psychiatrist's signature for documents attesting to Sean/a's mental and physical struggles—which would qualify her to obtain things such as veteran student debt forgive-ness—has been a unique challenge.

Ironically, as we waited in yet another physician's office who was unwilling to sign off on her documentation because she hadn't been a long-term patient (most homeless people aren't getting routine medical care!), Sean/a noted that the physician who owned the entire group of clinics had been a friend of hers. In fact, she'd hired Sean/a to coach her kids decades earlier. Sean/a remembered the physician's husband and recalled having dinner at their house.

It struck me that if Sean/a couldn't even get a simple document signed by someone with so much clout in the medical community who could vouch for her, and with me as a (somewhat forceful) advocate and ally, how in the world would anyone without such support even begin?

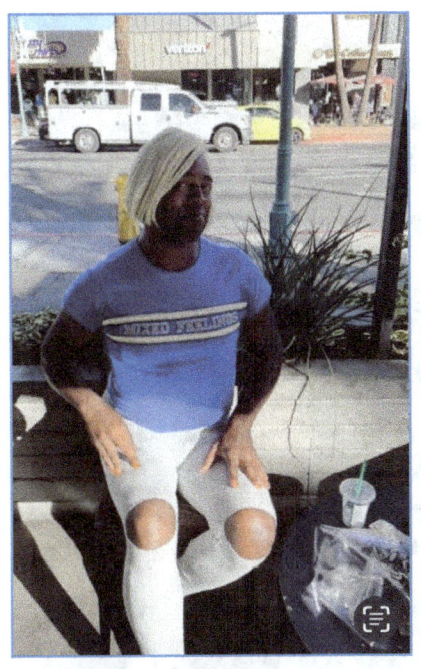

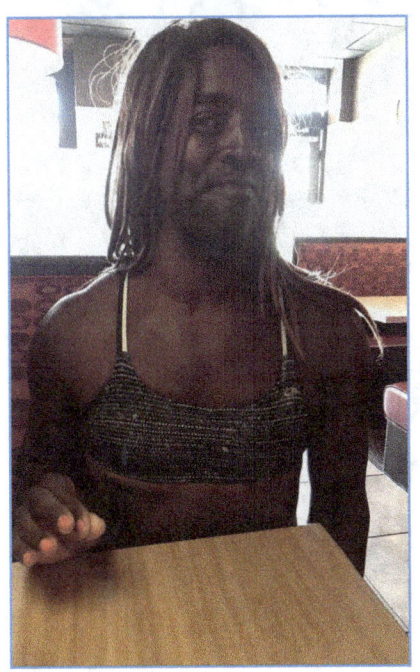

The freezing shower Sean/a used for 8 years.

CHAPTER 5

Category of One

"*I always knew the limits of what I could handle. It's like being in the weight room; you have to know how much weight you can shoulder. I have been challenged to grow and expand. When someone said, 'Here, Sean/a, let me help you,' there were days I felt like I couldn't trust for fear of being hurt. I knew on those days to accept my limits. Other days, I felt the courage to step out of my box and give someone a chance by saying yes, I will listen and have faith.*"

~ Sean/a

Unforgettable. Unmistakable. That's who he/she/they are.
Here she came just walking down the street, singing "Hi, Doc." Her tall, athletic, insanely-sculpted-through-years-of-exercise self bounced joyfully toward me for one of our weekly meetings at the local Juice Crafters. Sean/a defied all expectations.

It seemed the entire street was either honking their horns, shouting, "Hey, Sean/a!" or stopping to just take her all in. A feast for the senses.

She wore a beautiful red sundress, oversized round sunglasses, and a wig of long curly blonde hair. Toting a quilted pink purse and bright-white sports sneakers, she transcended assumptions and asked simply to allow herself to be fully known on her terms, free from biases and stereotypes.

She eagerly ordered her usual—a Brazilian acai bowl—and we sat down in a table for two near a large window. We made quite a pair. With her huge, infectious laugh and my broad smile in her presence, it felt as if we were in a positivity bubble all our own that everyone around seemed to notice. The nonalcoholic fizz Sean/a generated felt like the best panacea for boredom or the mundane.

We had barely sat down, much less started our conversation, before an elderly woman approached the table. "How ARE you?" Sean/a asked the woman.

"You look lovely in blonde," the woman said.

"You're so kind." I noticed Sean/a spoke softly, enunciating her words more precisely than usual for the sake of this woman. After the conversation ended and she walked away, Sean/a turned back toward me. "Lady I've known for years." She laughed. "Wonderful soul!"

I found it a remarkable experience to simply observe the interactions between Sean/a and the people of La Jolla. Sean/a never seemed to miss a beat, calling most folks by their names—from newfound friends she'd recently met to old-timers she'd known for thirty years. It hit me that there didn't seem to be one among them untouched by her essence.

I was about to speak when she jumped up. "Give me a sec." Sean/a sauntered over to an athletic man in his fifties, dressed like an obvious mover and shaker, sitting a couple of tables over.

"Hey, what's up?"

The man reached out and shook her hand. "Sean/a, how you been?"

"Doin' great, thanks, and you?"

They exchanged a few words, and I took note of the unique way she adjusted her voice and personality to connect with whatever person was in front of her—like she was in ultimate resonance with their being.

She sat back down in front of me, a broad smile on her face. "I'm so blessed, I can't say it enough."

"You know you really have to tell your story," I said while I had her attention. "The wonderful people of La Jolla should know it."

She laughed loudly. "Yeah, Doc."

"I'm serious," I told her. "The world should know your story. People are always curious about you when they see you. You have a magnetism that draws them in, but they only know bits and pieces."

Her acai bowl, which had arrived while she was chatting with the athletic man, sat in front of her. Too busy interacting with others, she hadn't even noticed it. "Your lunch," I reminded her.

She gathered her napkin and took a ladylike bite, then set down her spoon. "My story, huh?" She paused, a thoughtful look on her face.

"Yes." Once I said it, I was even more convinced that the magnetic force of Sean/a's personality and her courage to live out loud, authentically in her truth, could inspire, help, and heal many.

"Okay." She smiled, then laughed, gifting me with her full presence and rapt attention. "Let's write a book. You wrote a 486-page dissertation, Doc. You can do this." She laughed again and then got serious.

"We," I said. "We will tell your story. Together."

Already, I could see the power of her reach. The tour de force of her energy. Once she'd publicly transformed from Sean to Sean/a, this energy of hers was liberated for full effect. And it clearly brought out the best in those around us. The cashier who took our order. The man who jumped out of his fancy sports car to wave hello.

"It's like you make each person feel as if they are your favorite person on earth," I remarked.

"Oh, maybe they are. What can I say? They fill my cup to the brim with love." She spread her arms wide. "I love the people of La Jolla!"

I felt grateful for being granted this view through the kaleidoscope of Sean/a's daily existence. She never minded an intrusion or interruption to our conversation, always looking up with a smile to see who was greeting her. I was curious whether she ever struggled with the attention, though.

"Are there days you just want to opt out of the spotlight?" I asked.

She shrugged. "Of course." Then she added, "But it goes with the territory of being Sean/a and I embrace it."

A woman, balancing a tray on one hand and holding a little girl's hand with the other, paused by our table. "Sean/a, that sundress fits you perfectly."

"Lilian, thank you! And look at your shoes. I love Uggs!" She let out a squeal of delight.

I sat, a silent witness of the humility, grace, and poise she exuded. Her general countenance made it clear she took neither her friendships nor the attention she received from others for granted.

After the woman passed by, Sean/a gestured with her spoon toward nothing in particular as she met my gaze. "You know, maybe a book is the way to go. Everyone thinks they know me, but they'll get a better sense of who I am."

"Are you okay with that?" I asked. "I know you like your privacy."

"There is a place for privacy and discretion," she conceded with a nod. "But you know me. I love connecting with people. Knowing everyone makes me feel like I'm an ambassador for the community."

I wondered if the exuberance she manifested in her wholehearted interactions with others was tiring. Sometimes, perhaps, those exchanges took more out of her than she even realized. At the same time, I recognized this was an aspect of her journey toward self-acceptance and belonging. My part was to be a supportive friend and companion on the journey.

"You make a great ambassador," I said.

"Thanks, Doc." She returned her attention to her bowl for a few moments, then set her spoon down once more. "Well, I don't smoke, I don't drink, I don't gossip, I don't gamble. I just go through life feeling blessed and so grateful. I love my life and the people in it. I can't say it enough, really."

"That's a terrific attitude to have," I agreed, although my mind was beginning to race. A book. Yes, Sean/a's story needed to be told.

"Hey, Doc, maybe we can turn it into a movie. Sometimes people just need to believe anything is possible. In Hollywood, and La Jolla," she said with an inspired twinkle in her eye, "dreams really do come true."

Sean/a continued, "My elementary school teacher told me once, 'Sean, when you grow up you are going to be a teacher and an entertainer.' I think he was spot-on."

I forced my attention back to the conversation. I could figure out the details of the book and the publishing industry later. Sean/a rarely mentioned her background, so I jumped at the chance to find out more about a teacher she'd never mentioned. "Do you remember anything else from this teacher?"

Sean/a was quiet for a minute, looking out the window at passersby. "He told me we all think too much. He said, 'Sean, let things be.' I never forgot that."

"What does letting things be look like for you?"

"Definitely not doing nothing!" she exclaimed. "It is vital that we all take every opportunity to be in service and to give back."

Her voice grew louder, and I felt like she wanted others to hear her message. "Trials and tribulations, fortunate and blessed, tested beyond what we can take in—but it's all for a purpose. When I was homeless, I knew there was more. I knew things were going to work out in the end. It just wasn't time … yet."

"And you're always finding new ways to give back." Even when homeless, Sean/a had shown herself as a good neighbor. Since becoming housed, she had become a volunteer community liaison to the homeless and was doing her part to assist the San Diego Police Department in that respect.

Sean/a straightened, a smile breaking through. "Oh, yeah! Helping other homeless people by offering them apples and oranges on my daily walks is my way of saying, 'I see you; you are never alone.' There are resources for people who want to get help in the crisis they are facing if they give it a try."

I shook my head. "It's incredible how you turned your experience into something positive. Do you ever feel overwhelmed by it all?"

Sean/a took a deep breath. "Sometimes, but I'm grateful for every step that brought me here. I want to tell people going through their own hard times that they will get through it if they never stop believing in a better tomorrow, if they trust there are good people out there who can help. I did."

"You did," I agreed, nodding. I loved how she approached every encounter with a ready smile and by asking how she could be of service.

"You know, I think a book is a great idea!"

"Let's do it."

CHAPTER 5

People needed the opportunity to meet Sean/a beyond our little enchanted village. She remains truly one of the most unique people I have ever encountered.

~ ~ ~

As I began to consider the building blocks of a book and started piecing Sean/a's story together, I recognized her connection with others as a powerful thread of her story. There was a mutual compassion, an interest and curiosity in her approach to others, that was truly heartwarming. Such mutuality is the essence of a healthy community.

I first felt an affinity for Sean when I moved to La Jolla, long before I witnessed his transformation into Seana. I noticed him at the local tennis courts for hours on end. As a muscular, six-foot, five-inch African American male, he stood out on the courts. At the time, I was married to a former professional tennis player. I noticed Sean's athleticism with interest and wondered if Sean and my husband, a Trinidadian American, might get a match in some day.

I also became aware of Sean's gregarious, affable nature when I realized the entire tennis club knew him. This was long before I found out that the club manager had quietly provided Sean with winter clothing and assistance for years. Just one of many people in the community who had shown deep kindness and whom Sean also repaid by promoting their businesses and serving as a very able-bodied helper, when needed.

Sean's athleticism was also noted at the basketball courts of the La Jolla Rec Center where he gave informal lessons to patrons' children and could be heard offering positive words of encouragement to those who frequented the center.

Whether as Sean or Sean/a, her connections with people stretched across the town of La Jolla, where she created memorable moments for close to thirty years—even during the eight years unhoused. The daily disappointments and seemingly impossible tasks of living homeless were rechanneled and sublimated into acts of service with mutual benefit.

Mutuality was evident in so many stories Sean/a shared. Local taco shops, bagel shops, and pizza parlors giving her the last pie for the day out of the back door, or the morning bagel, or a breakfast burrito. A local business providing Sean/a with a mattress she could tuck away wherever she found space to rest—a big step up from the cardboard she had been sleeping on. In return, she always managed to offer some kindness, which kept the community circle flowing, uninterrupted.

I contemplated Sean/a's overall approach to her interactions with others. Even in negative circumstances, her responses were usually positive. Not once did she yield to the temptation to lash out when provoked by teenaged tourists—white males who threw beer cans at her from their car speeding past on the street—or those who would mock and imitate her at a local carwash, calling her derogatory names. Nor did she succumb to anger when faced with injustice on the city bus when people harassed her for information or insulted her with sexual innuendos.

These interactions affected her in other ways, often deeply, and she developed a manner of coping that wasn't always understood by those around her, which we'll get to in a later chapter on mental health. Overall, however, she allowed those who respectfully engaged with her to enter a vast, more soulful realm of experience. A place where they could find moments of connectivity.

The potential for healing divisions based on race, class, gender, and mental health was revealed and constellated through Sean/a's exceptionally patient and understanding nature. Yes, her story needed to be told—the ways in which she accessed the grace to rewrite the script of her existence which allowed her to redirect her energy inward and upward.

I reflected on what it was that drew so many people to Sean/a. Part of it, at least, was the way she does things in the right spirit, transcending assumptions, biases, and habitual ways of seeing. Her sacred self—in deep resonance with her innermost self—emerges with something real and fresh in each interaction.

The positive attitude she maintained was in many ways due to her deference to a greater power at play in the universe. These were the qualities that compelled me to dive right in to help her on that rainy night. But the conversation had since expanded. The "plot had thickened" to include my witnessing her soul's evolution as it was unfolding in real time.

As Sean/a, she was embracing an aspect of herself that had previously not been accessed while she was Sean. She was bravely showing up with an identity that was being revealed to herself even as she was manifesting that self, day by day.

How often we pass through life unaware of how vitally interconnected we all are! Truly, what goes around comes around, and this was something Sean/a intrinsically recognized. She understood the role of her own free will and admitted that she made mistakes along the way, yet her humility and devout faith in something greater drew us together in a quest toward reclaiming Sean/a's dignity.

The journey was not merely a physical one. It involved not only getting her permanently off the streets but also into a solid place of self-acceptance, and that, I realized, was an ongoing struggle. If anyone was up to the challenge, though, it was Sean/a, who has repeatedly had to start over in life.

Rather than allow herself to be pulled under by obstacles, she simply began where she was, in the here and now, and moved forward. She determined her starting points, uncovered her goals and dreams through daily journaling and structured meditations that removed blockages, and identified strategies that would enable her to move purposefully through life. Cultivating such growth has been one of Sean/a's gifts to the community.

Sean/a honors the notion of a higher unity of events guiding and propelling her forward; this concept involving the harmony of all things connected yields unshakable confidence and wisdom that Sean/a loves to talk about with all who will listen. She embodies the adage by revered psychologist William James that in order to effect change in one's life, one must start immediately and pursue it flamboyantly, with no exceptions.[4]

Her connection to a divine source of truth and light is part of what gives Sean/a her illuminated, almost rapturous glow. These inner Divine sparks are supercharged and plugged into an other-worldly source. To her, the universe is a living presence to which she submits herself, and all else pales in comparison to the deep sense of peace and joy that infuses her soul.

Sean/a's expanded awareness and consciousness, coupled with her attunement to the Divine, allow for a synthesis of her life's events into a unified version of her history—one far greater than her personal narrative would allow. Numinous encounters with her True Self have promoted the miraculous, as her faith is consistently far greater than her fear.

By embodying the concept of simply taking the next right step, Sean/a has ended up where she intended to be … even though many steps along the path were dimly lit. Often, she hardly knew where to put her feet, but she marched bravely forward nonetheless.

4 William James, *The Varieties of Religious Experience: A Study in Human Nature* (Penguin Books, 1982).

CHAPTER 6

Intersex—
An In-Between Identity

"When I discovered I was intersex, the first thing that came to mind was shock!! How do I live my life as an intersex woman? One day at a time with lots of prayer. My sex is not M. My sex is not F. My sex is MF!! Anatomy/Physiology 101, please help!!

"There were long confusing nights in my soul, searching for the answers, but I knew the truth would come out, eventually."

~ Sean/a

As she sat in the doctor's office in La Jolla, nervously shaking her leg as if about to complete a hundred-yard dash, Sean/a's mind flashed back to her first appointment with Dr. Chen at the Gay and Lesbian Center. This doctor had finally confirmed to her what she had long suspected. She was, in fact, part male and part female—a condition known as intersex.

A few years had passed since then and Sean/a again found herself in a waiting room with nothing to do but wonder if the halls of medicine could help put her endless questions to rest. Could they teach her how to better understand this confusing body she had been born into? Could they help her navigate the even more confusing world, which didn't seem to have a place for in-between and/or/both people like her?

Society had offered little to make this complex journey any easier. She never understood why her medical condition, the obvious focus of fascination, was so inherently difficult for people to process and understand. This was another routine (and dreaded) visit to the doctor, which started off as straightforward and ended up leaving her feeling pathologized.

Sean/a was anxiously awaiting her lab results to get treatment for a routine infection. She had refused the doctor's request to subject her to an ultrasound to see the extent of her female organs and try to more completely understand her ambiguous genitalia. She attempted to explain to the doctor that it wasn't necessary, nor would it be healthy for her since she felt guarded and protective of her right to privacy.

At least at the Gay and Lesbian Center, they had offered solutions. There, she was met with compassion, along with offers of support groups and therapy.

Sean/a stepped outside for fresh air and started texting me about whether she should subject herself to imaging, knowing full well that no matter the result—vestigial uterus or not—she would likely be dissatisfied or even traumatized by the experience.

"Do you think it would serve a useful purpose for you?" I texted back.

"Not at this time," she responded.

Sean/a had been forthcoming about her condition to the newspaper in interviews during the Shelter for Shauna project. As with many other aspects of her life, as much as she wanted privacy, it appeared her identity was on display for public consumption. She felt that by telling her story in her own words, she would regain a semblance of control.

I'm sure the physician was not only doing her due diligence but also likely felt she was doing Sean/a a service by putting her queries to rest. However, due to the doctor's position of authority, Sean/a felt pressured to justify her condition.

I reiterated to her that, from everything I had read about being intersex, a person could define oneself as intersex by just believing one had male and female energy inside; that was substantial as far as the definition went.

"It's a new world, Sean/a," I texted. "Only you can define you."

Sean/a got her prescription and left. That was five years ago. And as far as I know, it was the last time she visited a doctor's office.

Some people, although curious about Sean/a, argued the veracity of her claim of having both male and female genitalia. The goading took her back to her childhood, reminding her of being teased and called names.

It no longer matters to her how she arrived at her current definition of self, her present identity. After suppressing Seana for fifty years of her life and at times feeling exhausted at manifesting as Sean, she was ready to embrace all that Sean/a had suffered in silence over the years. She was ready to allow herself the free expression she had long craved.

Intersex refers to people born with a range of conditions and characteristics that exist outside the traditionally conceived notions of male and female bodies. While some intersex conditions are identified at birth, others aren't diagnosed until puberty or later in life.

Medically defined as a group of conditions with a discrepancy between the external and internal genitals, being intersex is increasingly defined as a disorder of sex development. Sex is distinguished from gender, with the latter referring to social roles or identity.

Intersex conditions affect roughly 1.7% of the population (almost the same as the percentage of people with red hair). The question of whether Sean/a is genetically intersex and how this is phenotypically or genotypically expressed was not going to offer her the deep internal validation she had long sought. All that mattered to Sean/a at that point was her conviction that this was indeed a condition with which she identified.

Physical conditions aside, trauma alone has the power to create male and female alternate selves inside a victim of severe abuse, and many come to refer to themselves as "they." For Sean/a, this was long her reality which, until now, wasn't comprehensible to society at large. Thus, she suffered many humiliating taunts to "prove" her intersex identity.

In truth, a fully unified self with certainty, coherence, and permanence is a fictitious thing. It is an ideal based on collusion with the demands of others. Each of us is a conglomeration of so many things—genetics, experiences, chemical balances (and imbalances), memories, and more. The capacities and inner abilities we have, and with which we regulate a sense of worth, are what provide a template or organizing principle upon which we can then construct higher-order processes.

When a child's sense of worth or identity is deeply affected by trauma or other deep-seated negative experiences, this can have lasting effects on one's metacognition and synthesis of knowledge. The enormous pressure to silence oneself on multiple levels, internally and externally, is analogous to that of a long-term abuse survivor, in which so many internal parts of the self must go unnoticed for far too long.

At one point, Sean/a's emotional journey to understanding herself consisted of buying several pregnancy tests on a weekly basis. "Just to validate that I am female," she explained to me. Although it defied rational explanation (since it would've been an immaculate conception), pregnancy tests helped her resonate with accepting the female part of herself, having feminine concerns, and seeking a sense of belonging in her identity as Seana. She was poignantly expressive and almost tearful when embracing her stomach as she spoke, as if she were conjuring deeply soulful stirrings of what it would be like to carry a child in her womb.

As with everything else in Sean/a's life, experiencing the world around her as unfiltered as she does makes her privy to the most raw experiences. In this case, she fully embodies the feminine aspect in its most primal form.

For a while, as part of that ongoing quest to find belonging within herself, Sean/a felt she needed to accentuate her female parts by acts such as wearing a bra to highlight, not just support, her breasts. She then adapted her approach, understanding that it was honoring all parts of herself just to coexist, without the need for rationalization or vindication. She proudly wore her bright colors, form-fitting miniskirts and leggings, wigs, and ladies' flip-flops (even when they didn't fit)—vacillating between wigs and dresses, leggings and baseball caps, and everything in between.

Watching her from afar, it was clear to me that she had all the feminine affectations, mannerisms, and attributes. Even when no one was looking, this was a part of her demeanor. Sean/a wasn't trying to impress others or be purposefully demonstrative; it was just who she was.

These days, ten years into our friendship, I have seen her bloom with self-confidence, almost as if Seana emerged from her own adolescence into mature womanhood with nothing left to justify or to rebel against.

One day I asked her, "Hey, Sean/a, just curious, how come we aren't writing the book as 'they'?" I wanted to know if she would prefer to identify in that way.

Sean/a replied, "I guess I'm as much 'they' as 'they' come, Kirst. Hard to explain, but when I'm Sean, I'm Sean. His world, his 'his'tory. And then as Seana, she gets reminded by others more often than Sean of her place in the world. I think by calling myself 'they,' I might add to the confusion. I'm FULLY Sean and FULLY Seana. Each is important in his/her own right. Does that make sense?"

"Absolutely. It's all how you wish to be acknowledged and addressed. It takes the world a while to catch up anyway." I joked with her that using the pronoun probably makes editing the book easier, but also wanted to make sure she was happy with the choice. "This is your life. We want to represent you as close to your lived experience as possible."

"Yes, ma'am," she texted back a moment later. "Let's go with 'he/him' when we talk about a time in Sean's life and 'she/her' for Seana's. That makes sense. I don't want to add to anyone's misunderstanding; my life has been confusing enough to me!"

"Let's do that," I agreed, then laughed aloud at her next comment:

"We don't want to create obstacles. Can you imagine some dear old lady reading the book and telling her grandchildren that we got the grammar all wrong? A day in my life, Doc."

Nine years after she first told me how utterly validating it was for her to be in Dr. Chen's office, Sean/a proudly showed me her health record, which we had ordered from the medical archives. In addition to various lab results, it clearly said in the box marked sex: MF.

"Doc, you understand my SEX is MF. Not my gender. I know it's confusing, especially in the south, but this piece of paper means everything to me."

"I'm happy for you," I told her. "You must feel so seen and acknowledged."

"PRAISE! You have no idea. I'm so grateful the good Dr. Chen was willing to put it down as fact. I am both. Always have been, always will be. People just need to get used to the fact that Sean/a is in here to stay!!"

Sal, Sean/a's loyal friend from the local copy center, obliged her requests and sent her copies of relevant articles and documents on the topic of intersex. She meticulously placed them in binders and files so that she could offer "proof" of her condition, lest anyone, including herself, doubt her or invalidate Sean/a again.

Living between sexes and genders of both and neither causes confusion, at best, and personal and societal disavowal and harassment, at worst. Permission to have the fluidity of moving back and forth has been liberating. The freedom to live authentically in a world full of understanding is Sean/a's wish for all who defy categorization and live outside the margins of what is considered mainstream in society.

One of Sean/a's most pressing activist issues—creating awareness around gender reassignment surgeries and the potential harm inflicted—speaks to the confusion she experienced as a child. She has a driving passion to create awareness of intersex surgeries performed without consent, which is shockingly prevalent in all areas of the globe. These unnecessary and irreversible surgeries to make bodies conform to traditional notions of male and female can cause great harm to the individual. Physical pain, loss of genital sensitivity, scarring and sterilization as well as harmful psychological effects (as the assigned sex post-surgery might not match the person's gender identity) are now considered human rights abuses.

Some physiologically intersex individuals were forced to undergo gender reassignment surgery as young children and may not have been told of this fact, yet were always acutely aware that something felt incongruous regarding their identity. Many intersex individuals are truly intersex in their DNA, having both ovarian and testicular tissue.

Most intersex cases are not easily apparent, with the tissue more ambiguous and vestigial in origin. Thus, intersex people can truly be any gender and any sexual orientation. Hormonal expression driven by the genetic endowment determining sexual development can result in variation of overtly expressed characteristics; for example, genital ambiguity and various combinations of chromosomal genotype and sexual phenotype.

Horrifyingly, fetal screening for the intersex condition has sometimes resulted in pregnancy termination, which entangles social stigma with an actual medical risk to the fetus. Pathologization of intersex conditions by the medical communities creates a hostile environment rife with social and psychological discrimination, which violates the right to life of intersex peoples.

Thankfully, ethics and human rights standards have rallied to prevent selective abortions. The invisibility of intersex conditions is changing, slowly but surely. It's about time.

Some countries, such as Malta, now outlaw nonconsensual medical interventions modifying anatomy; the U.S. still allows a small group of specialists to perform such heinous procedures. Autonomy over one's own body should be an inalienable right, yet parents are often pressured into making irreversible decisions before a child can participate in the discussion, leading intersex people to experience lifelong harm as a result of the assumptions of others.

Respecting privacy is paramount, as is respecting the pronouns or gender identity a person chooses. Some intersex people go by "ze/zir" to reflect the inclusive him/her, he/she, they/theirs. Although intersex is not the same as transgender, Sean/a often notes the more visible transgressions against the transgender community as impetus to protect the rights of intersex and trans communities from harm and violence.

As intersex designates one who is born with a variation in the internal or external sex characteristics, transgender defines a person who identifies with a different gender than assumed at birth, with the sex characteristics usually conforming to generally understood male or female genitalia, unless WILLINGLY surgically altered. Both communities often suffer from misunderstanding and a loss of authority over their own bodies. Unwarranted or unwanted surgeries do occur in each group, with transgender individuals often pressured into conforming to their gender designation on identification documents.

Even though intersex is somewhat rare (one in roughly two thousand people have ambiguous genitalia), it is a constant in Sean/a's life to have to prove to herself and others all aspects of her existence, not the least of which is her sex. Imagine having to justify your basic existence as "valid" on a daily basis. Would you not also be confused and outraged?

As inhumane as strangers' comments can be, however, they give Sean/a the opportunity to perform what she considers her fundamental role in society: to be an advocate and to educate, as well as to protect vulnerable others like herself from harassment, bullying, and abuse.

Sean/a garners respect in the community and from those around her by standing firm in her beliefs and her steadfast devotion to self-expression, believing at her core that she has the right to freely exist as she wishes. Because she respects the universal rhythm, Sean/a invites her community to mirror her highest aspirations and thus eradicates any self-limiting beliefs.

In learning to be unapologetically genuine and true to herself, she actively reframes perspective and invites others to that same vista.

It hasn't been easy, though.

One evening, as we were chatting over the phone, the topic of identity came up.

Sean/a stated, "The opportunity to be myself and show others who I really am has been a natural challenge with the fact that I'm the only one in my different arenas."

"What arenas are you referring to?" I asked.

"Well, I'm an African American, intersex female in affluent, predominantly white suburbs." She laughed. "I am reminded of getting a sports scholarship to a white college, growing up very tall, just learning to accept whatever clothing fits."

"But you were also class president and class treasurer," I reminded her. "Don't forget that."

"It's always been about getting in where you fit in and acclimating, yet also standing proud in my uniqueness. They say 'it's lonely at the top.' I have no one to compare myself with."

"So, does that mean you're lonely?"

She hesitated a moment before answering, "I'm full of gratitude. I have learned to love myself as a 6'5" African American female athlete, PE teacher and coach, who happens to be formerly homeless, intersex, and single, but connected to many."

Ah, that's Sean/a. She really does have the heart of a coach—a mentor and teacher facilitating open dialogue and connection with the intent to teach and inspire. She doesn't have a problem attaching herself to all of humanity. Her embrace of each stranger as a cherished member of a global community magnetically draws people to her. For the most part, they leave their interactions with her uplifted and buoyed by her sense of possibility.

She heralds social change in her interactions with one individual at a time. As Sean, he portrayed an enthusiastic, patient, nonjudgmental example of perseverance through hardship and unselfconscious well-being.

As Seana, she became a heightened ambassador for all the categories she represents. Suddenly she became a political lightning rod, thrust further into the spotlight for merely existing. She was called names, told she was a menace and too flamboyant. Yet she learned to fully embrace an empowered feminist perspective.

She was tired of being the butt of jokes, feeling like her life was a constant April Fool's Day. Sean/a's good nature allows her to laugh at herself. But for the right reasons.

Sean/a is an active participant in rebuilding the mystery of her life as she remains open and curious and rejoices in her soul's wisdom unfolding. Her childlike curiosity and playful leadership, asking and answering all queries with an open mind, keep her poised to learn from all interactions.

Feminism highlights how exclusion from social mobility has for so long been a matter of gender, and that a new, inclusive narrative is vital for recovering the voice of the disenfranchised. Sean was often invisible, and he fell through the cracks, exiled and homeless. As Seana, she was visible and people were more apt to help, with the caveat that she stayed humble and deferential. The constraints of gender ethics were entrenched, and Sean/a still spends an inordinate amount of time straddling the cultural divide.

Her insatiable desire for joy allows her to remain open to purity and transparency, which together act as guides to Sean/a in living her authentic truth. Sean/a's courageous and compelling account of living as both male and female (yet having been unaware of her condition for much of her life) begs us to show understanding and offer inclusion.

Finally coming to understand herself as intersex answered long-unsolved conundrums in Sean/a's mind—the internal sense of her soul being both male and female. Gender fluidity and nonbinary are just some constructs that can help close the comprehension gap and name the sense of being internally occupied by another self of the opposite sex and the ability to move back and forth.

I suspect that as in all things, a holistic approach that reminds us that we are all part of something greater and magnificent and that all of the grandeur is also within, applies with sex and gender as well. The discrete differences and categorical teasing apart feel necessary and validating, as no two people are truly the same. Such is also the case with limiting descriptive designations on sex and gender. We all beg to be holistically seen as so much more.

~ ~ ~

The connection Sean/a has to her essential self is her most awesome responsibility; here, she manifests an allegiance to enlightenment and transcendence. Recovering peace, balance, happiness, and connection with her innermost essence, her true identity, has given her the capacity to transmute pain into healing.

It's a new world these days: at times, very intolerant and bigoted; at others, open-minded and accepting. Many youths of today have heralded tolerance, forcing older generations to address ongoing ambiguity and confusion regarding labeling. So many people, both young and old, are working to create awareness of the damage that can unfold if people aren't careful and sensitive to identity issues.

Sean/a is one of these people, and I am grateful for the work she is doing—both for herself and for others. Understanding that she is personally accountable for her own evolution, she keeps moving forward despite the challenges. In her bravery, she manifests beauty, intention, and purpose regardless of her circumstances. Her heart is her personal north star, and she stays true to her rules within.

In undertaking the process of soul retrieval and uncovering her soul's destiny, Sean/a is reclaiming the power once taken from her. Every time she dictates the course of an interaction—whether in a physician's office or a therapy group—she fortifies her sense of control. Her courage invokes compassion, and her compelling vision invites all those who are inspired to follow her lead on the journey.

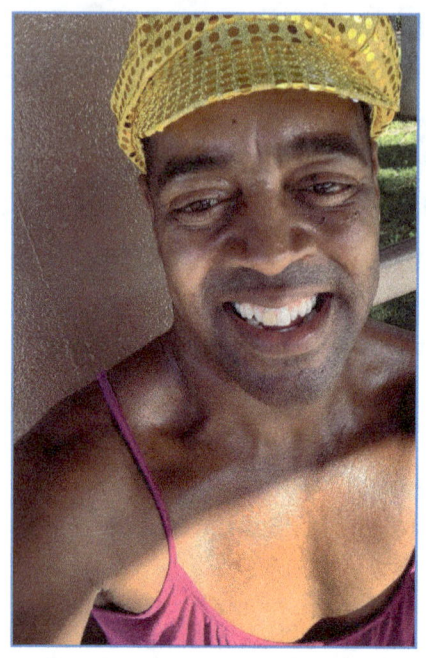

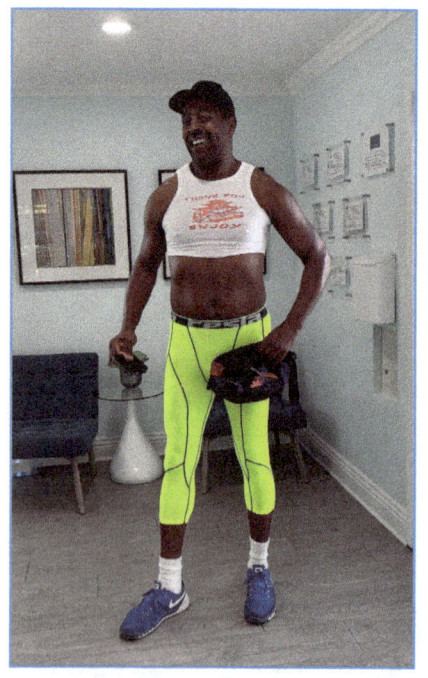

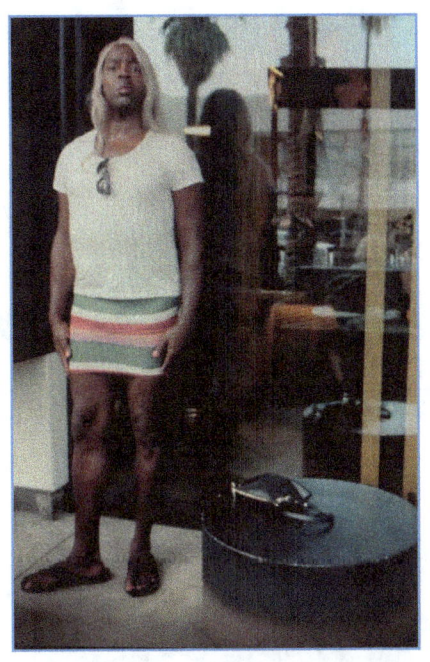

CHAPTER 7

Synchronicities

"When it comes to absolutes, how do we really know? You don't need a lot of proof; you don't need to know for sure; you just need to know that you believe. I know when something is going to happen. I sense it."

~ Sean/a

I wonder what Sean/a is doing right now?

The thought abruptly came to me as I drove down the street, approaching an intersection. I took a right turn and there she was.

It wasn't the first time this had happened. Already once that week, I had just been thinking about her when she turned the corner and almost ran into me. In fact, it had happened with such undeniable frequency that I was feeling a little like the character Samantha from the old seventies TV series *Bewitched*. It felt as if I could just envision Sean/a, and she'd appear seemingly out of nowhere.

We met up at Juice Crafters a few days later. These synchronicities were on my mind, and I jumped right in.

"How is it that you 'just happen' to be in the exact place and time when someone is thinking of you?"

"I don't think I have some special power," she responded after a moment of thought. "First and foremost, I know someone is always watching over me. Maybe that is what guides the direction I take sometimes, when someone is also thinking of me who possibly needs a reminder that we are part of something else together."

"I surrender my disbelief around you, you know?" I told her, taking a sip of my Green Soul Smoothie.

Her expression remained preternaturally calm, like she was not the least bit surprised at my words. "Even though people aren't right in front of me sometimes, I feel they are with me. Faith is not seen; it's just there and it is really important to me."

I shook my head. "It makes no rational sense to me, or to others. Sometimes it feels like you are conjured out of the ether."

With a twinkle in her eye and her head turned ever so slightly, as if enraptured by an otherworldly chorus, Sean/a's entire being appeared aglow—lit from within and without simultaneously.

"You want to know the strangest part?" I continued.

"Tell me, Doc," she said with a smile.

"I said this to the teller at the bank, and the baker at the gourmet bakery nearby. Both of them stopped what they were doing and looked at me like I was reading their minds. Seriously, they both said something like, 'That is so crazy. That happens to me with Sean/a all the time as well.' I guess none of us can explain it."

I have wondered at times if Sean/a is a walking spirit, fully connected and open to the invisible yet transcendent field. The spiritual implications of what she has survived and how her apparently "disintegrated" mind may actually be fully integrated and connected to a higher plane of existence—tapping into the ground of all consciousness—boggles the mind.

For some, in attempting to make meaning and find solace during lonely and alienating events, or during times of great psychological agony, the mind appears to tap into a restorative energetic field. This inexplicable ability has been substantiated by quantum physics, mysticism, near-death research, and work with dissociative conditions.

I took Seana/s "coincidental occurrences" as validation that she was somehow wired to be receptive to another dimension in a way that most people simply aren't as attuned to.

One of the strangest examples of this was when I was in a park in Santa Monica with my daughter watching squirrels scamper up a tree. My daughter and I had never discussed squirrels before or paid much mind to them before this day. I mentioned to my daughter how the sight reminded me of my childhood in Minnesota.

Out of the seeming blue, I got a photo from Sean/a *of a squirrel.* No context or explanation. I was flabbergasted, but I probably shouldn't have been surprised in the slightest. After all, things like this have happened hundreds of times with her over the years.

A fellow La Jollan and friend of Sean/a, Richard, also mentioned this uncanny, almost prescient noticing—a thought about Sean/a— that would result in her being right around the corner in a "random" encounter. This happened so frequently he started to refer to these experiences as having a "Sean/a feel" and would consistently ask himself, "Why did that happen?"

Richard and I went to lunch at the Museum of Contemporary Art and spent an hour discussing quantum ideas as they related to Sean/a. The most bizarre aspect of the conversation was that both of us had felt strong hunches about the nonlocal nature of these "coincidences" with Sean/a, yet neither of us had spoken of them aloud to anyone before because the mere thought sounded so implausible.

It was truly extraordinary that while conversing about our mutual friendship with Sean/a—which had brought Richard and me together in dialogue—we arrived at the same conclusion: There is something inarticulate about her, almost telepathic in her awareness and how she then transmits that knowing back to whomever she is with.

"People need to be asking not what's wrong with her, but what's right with her," Richard said at one point in the conversation.

His statement struck me with its profound truth. "That's it!" I told him. "You're spot-on."

Acting as a spiritual conduit of sorts, Sean/a is in touch with an energetic current or vibration that few access in their lifetimes. Whether it be out of sheer survival, a brain wired with increased right-temporal-lobe activity and its integration of sensory experiences and emotion, connection to a "God spot" or mystical portal, or just a deep attunement to others, she seemingly embodies a profound attunement to the transcendent nature of reality.

Healing power from a divine source of love seems to palpably flow right through Sean/a into whomever she touches.

So I'm sure you might be saying to yourself, "Well, this happens to everyone at times." And YES, glimpses of the Divine order are ALWAYS peeking through, waiting to be recognized as such. It's hard to convey, however, the almost surreal quality to the frequency and intensity of these moments with Sean/a which beg to be acknowledged in their full spiritual expression.

This isn't an easy thing to write about because it's not an easy thing to understand and convey. At first, I was hesitant to share this aspect of Sean/a with others as it can come across as unbelievable.

This isn't a work of fiction, after all. But I believe those who are willing to venture forth into this uncharted territory will find that companionship, compassion, and loving kindness are the treasures that make the trip worthwhile.

~ ~ ~

While discussing these matters with Sean/a, a light came on for me. Her perceived encounters with the Divine in everyday life as well as during her severe psychological traumata illuminated an interesting overlap with those who have had spiritual awakenings during events such as near-death experiences and peritraumatic dissociation.[5]

Insights gleaned from her visits to the imaginal, when viewed phenomenologically, inform how the soul can survive the unthinkable and return with otherworldly protection from guardian spirits, invisible allies, and self-helpers to guide, comfort, and protect.[6] The Inner Self Helper described in a future chapter comes again to mind. The presence of this coordination center of these unseen allies is more readily acknowledged during altered states of consciousness.[7]

To the untrained eye, Sean/a might have appeared to be all ego. Living large, out, and proud. Yet to those intimately acquainted with her, the truth of her full self-investment into the caring aspects of human relationships gave her a presence few can realize. Her utter loss of control in managing the basics of her survival translated into far greater control as she subjugated herself to a vast wisdom and power: the universal spirit, which she calls God.

---

5 Peritraumatic dissociation (PD) describes a range of psychological reactions that can occur during or immediately after a traumatic event, including depersonalization, derealization, dissociative amnesia, altered time perception, and out-of-body experiences.
6 Donald Kalsched, *The Inner World of Trauma: Archetypal Defenses of the Personal Spirit* (Routledge, 1996).
7 Jeffrey Raff and Linda Vocatura, *Healing the Wounded God* (Nicolas-Hays, 2002).

Deeply listening to all that Sean/a's inner voices had to say connected me more fully to the mystical aspect of life. Her expanded powers of awareness gave her the ability to translate the details of her life and string the nuances together to create meaningful action in the community. This was a process of continual ego surrender and reinstatement.

I'm sure there are many readers (including my Cambridge-educated, grounded-in-Newtonian-physics father) who might say, "Okay, you've lost me here" in these musings. However, there is something so inexplicable about the nature of these encounters that I would be remiss if I didn't include them in a book about her life and impact on the world at large.

Sean/a tells me that I was born with the gifts of encouragement and hope. I would say she was born with the gifts of optimism, perseverance, and faith. The overlap of our personalities uniquely suited us to the task at hand; namely, to find Sean/a shelter and restore her dignity while being cognizant of her wish to not alter the fundamental truth of who she is.

Conformity was not a choice.

Living outside of categories seemed to define her life. Honoring her true Essence, her oversoul that appeared to direct her at every turn, allowed Sean/a the freedom to choose the life she wanted according to her own principles. And she has indeed been chosen. To make a difference.

Although I'm sure she's had moments of self-consciousness and insecurity in her process of transformation, what strikes me the most is how Sean/a stands solidly in her truth. She is, to me, a modern-day Rosa Parks, with an ethereal wisdom that imparts strength of conviction with otherworldly protection.

The journey to heal from and integrate profound wounding, and the resultant spiritual insights, continues throughout one's lifetime and perhaps beyond. As a therapist, I am constantly reminded of the power of the therapeutic alliance and how this can make or break the therapy. It requires wisdom to understand that trauma often occurs in the context of relationships; thus, healing requires a healthy, new, relational foundation.

Deep friendship is the balm that makes all the difference. It is based on choice and unabashed acceptance.

The Divine is made manifest in loving interactions. When Sean/a and I are together, it's as if the forces of our individual subtle bodies amplify to such a degree that the energy radiates in an ever expansive field, highlighting and illuminating possibilities. People around us get caught up in the fervor, buoyed by our connection and the generative energy we have co-created.

Sean/a showcases her resilience in her capacity to find meaning in traumatic crises and then to use ensuing spiritual conversions to reprioritize her goals and seek to engage in virtuous behavior. Showing forgiveness, expressing gratitude, practicing humility, and displaying compassion and wisdom appear as hallmarks of the spiritually evolved human being whose goal is the betterment of the lives around him or her. Such people reveal the awesome interconnectivity of all things.

When one enters relationships as potential encounters with the soul, then a new creative formulation and harmony of perspectives results. This was EXACTLY what Richard, the banker, the baker, and I had all noticed; namely, that things around Sean/a just seemed to palpably shift in her presence. Things that hadn't previously made sense suddenly clicked into awareness properly. A certain energetic knowingness that she embodies had the ability to put our earthly concerns to rest when she was nearby.

The fundamental shift from doubt to wonder is an opening through which reverie and hospitality has the opportunity to enter. Creating space for these otherwise sealed-off voices often begins in people who experience them as a gift of survival, but they can develop into so much more. Enlightened souls such as Sean/a redefine normalcy; they help us connect, shift, and realign attitudes and beliefs.

New possibilities are imagined, and the path toward cosmological connectedness is forged.

~ ~ ~

Sean/a's internal network is a "third reality" that transcends ordinary conscious awareness and facilitates survival in an ofttimes harsh external reality. It has long been my contention from extensive research (and forty years studying trauma) that this third reality is nonlocal. In other words, it resides in the quantum field and not just in the individual unconscious.[8] If this nonlocality is indeed the case, it allows Sean/a's mind to tap into the universal mind with more ease than anyone I have ever encountered.

Multiple descriptions of reality are necessary to honor the complexity of our existence. Sean/a has opened my eyes to omniscience and possibilities beyond what can be seen; she is a living, breathing example of deep attunement. Sean/a walks through life in a constant state of wonder and awe.

When we allow ourselves to be humbled by that which we did not know (or were previously mis-attuned to), we receive the gift of being inspired by a new awakening, an insight that was previously obscured. By revering the wisdom that people such as Sean/a have gleaned from living a life outside of the normally circumscribed boundaries—both physically and consciously—we begin to realign our collective biases.

---

8 Kirsten Viola Harrison, *Understanding the Nature of Spiritual Encounters in Near-Death Experiences and Dissociative Identity Disorder* (Pacifica Graduate Institute, 2009).

Making the choice to learn from instead of reviling those who speak outside of our comfort zones shifts our perceptions and increases our comprehension. Assimilating a confluence of ideologies from a variety of disciplines and listening to marginalized voices liberates the soul.

I saw a post recently that stated that there are five types of people to surround oneself with for an enlightened life: the inspired, the motivated, the open-minded, the passionate, and the grateful.[9] It occurred to me, of course, that Sean/a was all five in one. I felt even more blessed.

Fostering a conscious relationship with the generative aspects of one's soul holds the potential to heal one's inner world. Concretizing our spiritual experience and making it manifest in the here and now acknowledges that a God-spirit has always lived within. The formation, recreation, and remembrance of self and soul—replete with emotion and meaning—gives us a greater capacity to embrace a wider field of restorative love.

Positivism and learned optimism teach adaptation and healing, leading to post-traumatic growth and neurological and psychological change. Learning how to evolve our thinking from those whose life experience—such as Sean/a's—is radically different from our own expands our perceptions and opens windows to new ideas and ideals.

The loving, compassionate outcomes of spiritual striving are an evolutionary bridge to the progression of humanity. Being deeply attuned to the voices of those, like Sean/a, who have experienced non-ordinary states of consciousness, exceptional human experiences, and suffering offers a cultural realignment. It is a paradigm shift in favor of hope, wisdom, and light.

---

9 "The Five Types of People to Surround Yourself With," NFICA blog, https://nfica.org/the-five-types-of-people-to-surround-yourself-with/

I think back to when Sean/a told me of the times she almost froze to death while homeless, not once but twice. I believe she used her mind, her dissociative and spiritual defenses, to create intact internal and external attachment systems as a sort of lifeline renewing her hope. She examined her core beliefs, perceptions, and faith and combined them with adult reasoning to fuel her very survival.

Despite being a survivor, she refuses to be a victim. Her egalitarian treatment of all, even those who have transgressed against her, neglected or bullied her, has kept her out of a victim stance.

~ ~ ~

In a recent encounter which can only be described as a synchronicity, I took an unplanned writing break to Gelson's grocery store, and who should I run into but Richard. After all these years. While working on this very chapter. It still confounds me, the universal timing of it all.

What is the likelihood? In the Sean/a-sphere, all things are possible. I'm a believer!

Humanity is forever indebted to individuals like Sean/a. Her great strength and courage have supported her journeys to the far reaches of human experience and awareness. People with gifts such as Sean/a's have shown themselves willing to risk personal privacy at great sacrifice in order that we—humanity at large—might evolve, learn, and grow.

Sean/a is consistently revising her inner narrative and continuing to heal by telling her story in greater context to an ever-larger audience, expanding her reach. Thanks to her joyful adoption of social media (which we'll discuss in the next few pages), her teaching has limitless impact.

Sean/a's profound experiences honor the voices in the margins. Among those who, like Sean/a, have at times felt abandoned, betrayed, and then comforted and nurtured by the Divine, there appear a set of phenomena, ideas, and insights proven to be transformative.

In mathematics, the theory of fractal basin boundaries describes that field just at the edge of chaos where everything becomes implicitly ordered.

Sean/a has striven to create order out of chaos and orient her whole being toward wholeness.

The role of the exceedingly helpful yet elusive ally, essence, witness, or spiritual helper as human-Divine bridge appears to be a construct validated by many who have elicited safety and comfort from this apparently compassionate universal energy. This essence may be the key to understanding the nature of the life-saving defenses of the spirit.

What is more, this transpersonal agent of transformation and guidance appears to be available to us all if we can learn to open ourselves to its presence. Thus, those who have traversed the edges of "sanity" may well become our best spiritual teachers.

CHAPTER 8

Technology—The Sean/a-verse

"I discovered, even with technology of the Obama phone in 2014, I was still stuck being Sean for some reason ... my only outlet and real resource was the village; but then along came the iPhone, apps, texting, and social media, and suddenly, like magic, the entire SEAN/A-verse opened up."

~ Sean/a

S ean/a sat hunched over, tiny flip phone in hand, one finger slowly pushing each number as many times as needed to arrive at the appropriate letter of the alphabet to spell a word. I sat, trying to be patient, as she tediously responded to a text.

Her little "Obama phone" had served her well, but technology had long moved on, and she needed to catch up.[10] She rarely used

---

10 Officially titled the Lifeline Program and administered by the Federal Communications Commission, the program that provided a free cell phone and subsidized data to low-income families was dubbed the "Obama phone" due to the popularity of the program during Barack Obama's presidency.

the old phone, but at least she could call a friend if she needed to, or make sure a local business was in need of her help before walking miles to get there.

When the world of texting had first opened up to her, it was a painstakingly slow, frustrating, yet liberating endeavor. Recovering from a childhood spent in speech therapy for a stuttering disorder had made the written word a safer, more reliable form of communication.

We had made it work for our local meetups around town, but I couldn't help speaking up again.

"You need a new phone. I think it's time for an iPhone, don't you?"

Sean/a had been pushing back on the idea of an iPhone for a year or more.

She paused from her texting and looked up at me. "I am so grateful for my Obama phone. I don't need anything else." Obama, the original community builder, surely showed his brilliance in making such lines of communication available for all. It served its function as a bridge back to society. Literal lifelines.

When she first received her simple phone from the San Diego Homeless Outreach team of the SDPD, she enjoyed the ability to connect but didn't have the numbers of many people to call. The phone was also limited in its features. Sean/a was comfortable with the tech she knew. The idea of it all being at her fingertips scared her. I got that.

Part of her had grown wary and a bit paranoid about being constantly monitored after so many years living freely "en plein air." She also didn't want to be exposed to a variety of paths to temptation she could potentially go down. Sean/a had discovered the hard way— when first learning about email—how she could get a bit carried away.

Most of all, it was overwhelming just how much technology had changed in the past decade.

When Sean/a had been homeless, she used to keep herself abreast of the news by planting herself in the La Jolla Library, slowly teaching herself to use its computers. When Lisa and David of the Water-Walking Foundation graciously donated a laptop to Sean/a, you would've thought she'd won the lottery. She proudly carried her laptop briefcase all over the place. She was quickly heralded into the computer age, learning to surf the web and other modes of communication that had eluded her.

While happy, she was also stymied by just how much was "out there." An iPhone would bring all that directly to her fingertips and fit in the palm of her hand.

When we bought Sean/a a "smart" television just after she got an apartment, she was transfixed by news and basketball. She also received a bunch of donated DVDs from her friend Sal and relished the ability to watch an endless stream of movies. Before long, she amassed an incredible DVD collection. We also secured her cable TV at the time, giving her the opportunity to watch games (including Kobe's last game, something she was thrilled to see, having been a collegiate basketball player herself).

Then one day, it happened. She agreed to try out an iPhone.

Now the world could be her oyster.

After a few weeks learning everything there was to learn at the Verizon store—with employees patiently answering her every fathomable question—she started discovering emojis, gifs, YouTube, games, movies, apps for everything … and suddenly it was like she'd entered her own virtual reality. Her expressive creativity went through the roof.

In fact, I am certain emojis were invented just for Sean/a!

She started learning text etiquette and realized quickly, much to her chagrin, that texting was to the point and not nearly as polite as face-to-face conversations. Interestingly, I hadn't noticed the charm and niceties that had flown out the window in the immediacy and efficiency of getting one's point across. Sean/a texted like a gracious Southern belle, always mindful of her proper diction and saying "please" and "thank you." (She still complains that few people say "You're welcome" via text.)

For Sean/a, this new world of texting and social media was like opening the window to her inner life. In our relationship, it allowed us to connect and understand each other much more readily. She popped up all over, larger than life, and was hard to ignore. As art truly imitated life, I became a devoted Sean/a-verse fan.

It seemed like a miracle conversion for her, this new world.

It was truly heartening to see her connect and come alive in this manner. A far cry from one tiny two-word text at a time (taking ten minutes to type with her fingers bigger than the whole keypad). Technology for Sean/a has been a godsend. Learning to text opened a giant new world for her. She found the ideal media to express her authentic voice and was immediately enraptured.

Sean/a spent hours on Facebook and social media. At first, she contacted all my friends, hoping to create an instant connection with people she had rarely met. I explained to her that there was etiquette and a cadence to growing these friendships, based on privacy and trust over time.

Soon, however, coaching and teaching became her primary goal in interacting with others online. She tirelessly posted and chatted to educate online communities by creating awareness of intersex struggles, anti-bullying, and homelessness. She also wrote often about the importance of faith. Ever the teacher, these topics grew to be the core of her myriad posts.

(As a personal aside, having raised a stepdaughter with special needs, watching her blossom with assisted technologies has made me exceedingly grateful to those who had the foresight and skills to invent an otherwise inaccessible portal to a rich inner world.)

Before long, Sean/a was sending me online news articles nearly every day. She was up for the challenge of learning how to do her banking, pay her bills, and sign her lease online. Whether it was looking up obituaries, alumni affairs, world events, or news—all those things she was once dependent on hearsay or physical newspapers for—she began to zoom around in cyberspace.

I was absolutely dumbfounded by the leaps and bounds she made with technology, far surpassing my own knowledge of social media. (And a far cry from the year I spent imploring her to accept an iPhone, assuaging her doubts and building up her confidence that she could handle it, and that technology would become her friend.)

Of course, it has. Everyone and everything are Sean/a's friends.

The impact of Sean/a's presence and her ability to become a part of and create community—whether in person or online—is astounding. Belonging to community at large and being a true world citizen seems to be her highest aspiration. But on her own terms. Sean/a is an innovator, recognizing how formulaic constructs of existing in this world don't necessarily stir the soul.

As one of the most natural grassroots organizers I have ever met, Sean/a faced no limits to her stratosphere of influence in cyberspace. She loaded apps on her phone and joined community subgroups and subcultures I never dreamed existed. As a watchful neighbor on the Riverside County Sheriff's office and the Palm Springs Police Departments' social media, she vouched for the local fire and sheriff organizations. On another platform, she kept tabs on sports clubs, and so on.

Paradoxically, the existential aloneness that some people feel while surrounded by many is an inherently foreign concept to Sean/a even as she's lived in solitude with no roommates or significant others and no family nearby. Somehow, she is quintessentially, simultaneously connected to the mundane, the multiverse, all of humanity, and the Divine. This resultant Lightness of Being fills her to the brim.

Sean/a has such an indestructible inner life that any voids in relationship she might experience, she amply fills with an expanded tether throughout the Sean/a-verse. Through her deeply rooted inner truth and conviction, Sean/a has not only discovered but learned to share her strengths and restorative love in the service of healing.

~ ~ ~

Recently, I felt my house shake and immediately received a text from Sean/a. "Doc, we just had an earthquake. My apartment shook, but I'm okay. Kinda scary. Luckily, I have the Quake App that warned me it was coming."

"Glad you're safe. I felt it, too," I texted back. Curious, I asked, "What would you say technology has done for you?"

After a few minutes, I got her response: "Technology has done so much for me to reconnect with friends from high school and college. It also affords me a platform to educate and show people a day in the life of Sean/a from my perspective. The opportunity to inform others about what it's like to be intersex has been a challenge on its own."

She causes tremors of hope and joy every day. If only people could learn to go along with the shifts instead of bracing themselves against them.

Sean/a was always early for our weekly appointments and showed up prepared anytime I arranged travel or meetings for her, but her sense of accountability was only enhanced by technology. Once she started using her iPhone regularly, her productivity—including weekly goals and affirmations she strictly adhered to—greatly improved.

While Sean/a's post-traumatic growth and thriving was evident in everything she did, the insights that these apps provided enabled her to become more emotionally and physically regulated. Even before embracing the latest technology, she consciously challenged herself to integrate new knowledge into her daily life; she grounded herself with routines, weekly meditations, and mantras. Sean/a utilized daily affirmations and set mental fitness and well-being goals for herself long before these things became part of the popular zeitgeist.

Once she discovered there were apps for those things, in her words, "Praise!" She loves accountability apps, which she has described as meditative and calming. They help her understand herself better by coordinating aspects of herself she hadn't previously brought together. Probably most important to her are the fitness trackers, which analyze her steps and the quality of her mood-walk therapy (more on that in an ensuing chapter).

The immediate feedback she receives from her smartphone's personalized data analytics grounds her in external life, acting as a reality check of sorts. Receiving awards on her phone from fitness apps and technology spurred her to become more focused on recognizing the somatic sensations most of us tune into automatically.

By tracking her daily habits and ideas, Sean/a utilized technology to make her aware of parts of herself previously unrecognized. I appreciated encountering her curiosity about it all, as she said to me (more than once), "Observation is so important." Her educational background and subsequent life experience—mingling with the far reach and depth of technology—served to combine all her knowledge into a giant forum, for which she has repeatedly expressed her gratitude.

What she regularly did in her walks around the community, Sean/a began to do online—allowing others to experience her optimism as she infused joy and hope in her many interactions. As a voracious learner and soul-searcher, she combines an examined life (her inner life) with a life of exuberantly interacting with people (her outer life), both in person and on the World Wide Web.

Even in cyberspace, Sean/a manifested her unique skill of bringing out the goodness in virtual strangers. Of course, the internet can also be a potentially dangerous place—with scammers and spammers, bullies and trolls. As you might imagine, people who disagreed with her on the issues she holds dear—such as the concerns of intersex people or those in the LGBTQ community—sometimes showed up on the platforms with inflammatory comments.

I was in awe of the caring that Sean/a showed even to those who attempted to taunt or dehumanize her. While some attempted to sever her from her life's narrative, or to minimize her experiences and challenges, they could not sever her connection to that soulful well of inner spiritual resources.

By virtue of her "superpowers," she often manifested that which she wished to create. In essence, she saw the good; as a result, abundance showed up around her in droves. People supported her and she continued to create that special kind of magic.

Instead of succumbing to trauma she suffered, Sean/a continued to fight for joy, cultivating it with hearty laughter and full, spontaneous expressions of awe and wonder. It was like she could access a greater realm of truth beyond the here and now—the Sean/a-verse—a part of the intangible, greater universe.

Her passion and excitement in those issues she felt strongly about were a giant spiritual "call to action." By engaging her social skills in person and via technology, she worked in the service of unity—hoping to shift the perspective of the collective toward understanding and tolerance.

This is something we might all strive to do in our own way. Instead of existing solely in echo chambers, communicating only with people who agree with us on every point, might we also put ourselves out there with joy, enthusiasm, and compassion? What would it look like if we sought to learn from others with curiosity and support others with our unique strengths? Deliberately expanding our perspectives and having the discipline to observe nonjudgmentally would facilitate the forging of new pathways—not only in the brain but on the roads that lie before us.

Both inwardly and outwardly, we have the opportunity to follow Sean/a's lead of inviting harmony with others instead of only tuning into our own small selves. In embracing mutuality as a vital component of equality, we increase respect, understanding, and empathy and thereby enhance communication and negotiation.

Online, just as in person, Sean/a was faithful to invest in the nature of love itself. She transcended the usual constructs (even if at times she sent out a few too many friend requests in her enthusiasm to connect with others). By putting forth peaceful invitations, she invited strangers and friends alike to join in discovering her many communities—physical and online—with fresh eyes and an open heart.

Her social, anthropological skills invited those around her to share a vision and join in her excavation of cultural truths seen with new insights and keen awareness.

Technology beckoned and she heeded its call.

Her appetite for adventure had only just begun.

It was time to take that hunger for new experiences to the next level.

CHAPTER 9

Traveling—Beyond the Comfort Zone

"Attitude is effort. God gave us a voice to use and actions to translate gratitude into allowing me to be myself. No one has it all together, especially me. I don't want to complain or argue or blame. I'm here today, I connect to life and am happy to say that this is who I am. I'm always ready to take the next step."

~ Sean/a

The texts from Sean/a popped up on my phone fast and furiously. "I feel like a real human being again! Can you believe I haven't been on a plane in SEVENTEEN YEARS?"

She didn't give me time to respond.

"Doc, It's like being born again, in a spiritual sense," she added. "My first flight in my life was at age seventeen from Denver to

Las Vegas. What a coincidence. You know I didn't sleep a wink last night."

When I read the next text, my eyes misted up. "Thanks for getting me out of my comfort zone, Doc. The world really is our oyster." This journey of Sean/a's had been a long time in coming, and it was worth it.

~ ~ ~

As Sean/a acclimated to life off the streets, I approached her with the idea of traveling. We started with what appeared to be a manageable itinerary: a day trip to San Francisco. It was a place where she would have the chance to experience LGBTQIA activism in action in a city known for its all-inclusive trailblazing and community spirit.

I had walked Sean/a through what she would have to expect from security—with its shoes-off policies and no walking of visitors to the gates. It was 2015, and she hadn't flown since 1998; much had changed, especially since 9/11.

She executed the entire trip flawlessly. In the weeks prior, we had gotten her an ID and she had her phone charged and ready to go.

Sean/a translated her adrenaline into excitement and followed the plan perfectly without letting her anxiety get the best of her. Still, I felt like a nervous mother dropping her child off at preschool for the first time. I was glued to my phone and hoped for constant updates and assurances even while not wanting to act like a hovering "helicopter mom."

She was faithful to provide those updates, letting me know that she had a great plane ride and expressing her astonishment at the advancements in air travel—from TV screens on the backs of seats to the TSA's careful security checks to portable credit card machines for snacks.

I had arranged for a local tour guide named Rick to take her on a full-day, personal, guided tour of the city. Sean/a loved it! Her joy at every magical corner of the city by the bay radiated out of her spirit. She was fascinated with Rick's tour, and the two of them enjoyed lunch together.

Clearly, Sean/a's special charisma rubbed off on him. I could sense his excitement as he got on the phone with me later and rehashed all the places they had visited and the local history they had covered. He stated that Sean/a was an absolutely unique pleasure, his "favorite customer." Her wonder and appreciation for every aspect of his tour had her mesmerized.

Rick took her to Stanford, where she had asked to visit the basketball courts, and then to various sports stadiums in San Francisco. She was in awe. Not surprisingly, she found a local Goodwill store and raved about the shoe selection for larger feet, which she presumed to be transgender sizes of women's shoes to fit men's feet in the Castro.

When she landed back in Southern California, Sean/a was so utterly enthused that she might as well have been coming home from a lunar mission; it was that foreign and wondrous at the same time.

Shortly thereafter, I planned another trip to San Francisco, this time with a tour guide, Sharon. I asked her to take Sean/a to Oakland and all the way up to Sacramento—a significant place for someone who lived for activism and representing intersex rights.

Perfectly poised with her back straight, standing even taller than usual, Sean/a proudly smiled for a photo outside Governor Newsom's office in the State Capitol building in Sacramento. She has a deep and abiding respect for the proactive and forward-thinking governor who was the first to honor gay marriage decades earlier. With her resume and a letter advocating for intersex rights in hand, she felt called to disseminate literature and educate those who had the power to fundamentally herald change.

Excited by the fact that Senator Mitt Romney had once kindly taken the time to walk the street with her in La Jolla and ask about her experiences, she felt emboldened to give her message a wider reach. Sean/a felt a kinship with the sense of inclusion for all and the open hearts that both Governor Newsom and Senator Mitt Romney conveyed. She deeply appreciated their wishes to grant all people the right to express themselves as they saw fit. Although sometimes on opposite ends of the political spectrum, the two men shared a deep humanitarian sensibility.

Sean/a had gone from living anonymously on the streets, homeless, to walking the halls of government, where she was undeniably visible. This was her moment.

The day added fuel to the fire in her heart for advocacy. She told me, "In Sacramento, I would love to make a difference, to be a leader and keep my head high and believe in something. I'd love to volunteer for Gavin Newsom and work for one of the sports teams. Teamwork. Inclusion. Belonging. It's everything."

Sharon also took Sean/a back to Stanford, the local sports arenas, and the greater Bay Area. Again, Sean/a made the most of every stop, checking out collegiate gymnasiums, posing for photos, and spending every minute engaged in conversation about history, politics, and tourism.

Eventually, Sharon drove Sean/a back to San Francisco, where I had booked her a hotel for the night. It was a completely new experience to use her own reservation and credit card to check in. After a few minor complications (and haven't we all had complications checking into a hotel?) she was exploring her hotel bedroom, complete with a king-sized bed.

"The most beautiful bed I've ever seen," she texted me.

And then, in a flash, she was out the door discovering the entire city on foot and by tram. By her enthusiastic series of text messages, you would think the gateway to heaven had opened. I received a flurry of updates—marveling at the colorful boutiques and beauty of the city. Her multidimensionality opened the door for each new adventure, which appealed to different aspects of Sean/a's nature.

Later, Sean/a told me how much she resonated with the spirit of place in the state capital. As a history buff who understands the power in standing up for one's rights, advocating, and making a difference, she honored her visit to a place where people worked hard in giving a voice to the voiceless—those like her who had been relegated to the margins of society.

But not anymore. Sean/a was living out loud and proud!

This trip led to a three-day excursion wherein she explored Chinatown, visited the college town of Berkeley, and rode on the BART. Sean/a told me she definitely left her heart in San Francisco. She lauded the sports community of the Bay Area, but what she loved most was the sense of belonging she felt there.

"I can be myself, no explanations," she stated. "It is a comfortable, intelligent, diverse area with a lot of Black heritage. Gay-friendly neighborhoods, great shoe shopping for size 16, women's shoes with heels. In San Francisco, I feel Sean is put to rest for a bit and Seana gets a new life."

Her text revealed something she rarely talked about (and definitely didn't dwell on or complain about) but that clearly still existed within her on some level: the challenge of finding where she belonged in that dichotomy between Sean and Seana. Yes, she was both, but sometimes it also seemed like she was, or perhaps felt like she needed to manifest as, one or the other. I imagined how exhausting such a constant tension might be.

But I didn't have much time to think about it. The travel bug had bitten, and we were often busy with travel arrangements of one kind or another. Shortly after that third trip to San Francisco, Sean/a took a train trip through Los Angeles up to Santa Barbara. She called it the most peaceful, relaxing trip she had had in her lifetime.

The call to action, however, kept nagging at her. She couldn't forget her short visit to Sacramento. It had sparked a fire of advocacy and activism that begged for more focused action.

Ever the researcher, Sean/a proposed a trip: What would I think about sending her as an intersex representative to Stonewall 50—the WorldPride event in New York City in June 2019? As the 50th anniversary of the Stonewall riots in 1969, it would be a series of LGBTQ events and celebrations, and it was the first time ever that WorldPride would be held in the United States.

I began to research it as well. San Francisco and Sacramento were both right here in California. New York was all the way across the United States. Would she be up for that long flight across the country? And the crowds in that vibrant city!

But we decided together that she would be up to the task and that there would be no better person to represent the intersex community than Sean/a. We jumped right into planning every aspect of the trip. LAX to NYC: This was the true test. We had discussed many journeys, ways for her to broaden her horizons from that corner perch outside Verizon on Pearl Street in La Jolla. Here she was, exhilarated at the prospect of exploring the city that never sleeps.

Sean/a texted incessantly from the moment she left her apartment, starting with a comment about the flight she would take—a direct flight from LAX to JFK: "OMG, a five-hour flight and no meal. Wow, how things have changed in airline travel in seventeen years."

"Doc," she then texted from the airport, "I hope I have an aisle seat. I'm six feet five and my legs are getting ready for that five-hour flight."

When she arrived in NYC, she proudly proclaimed herself as "Sean/a, the Southwest's intersex person rep."

And Sean/a was truly in all her glory.

A purple wig, bright pink top, and in the ultimate hotspot, Sean/a stood ten feet tall in her mind in Times Square. Blending seamlessly with all the other attractions, she felt at once completely visible—as if really seen for the first time—and yet just another part of the crowd, which was both unfamiliar and refreshing.

"There is so much human kindness here, true and rich culture, lots of Black people. I haven't felt alone once."

A few moments later, "It is mind-blowing, the architecture alone is astounding. And the pizza! They love pizza, and the smell is amazing."

I wasn't surprised at the rapid-fire texting. After all, it was her first time in New York City.

"They are ranking WorldPride with New Year's Eve," she messaged. "Thousands of police officers tackling hate crimes and 150 floats for the LGBTQI parade. It is historic. Unbelievable!"

I felt so grateful to receive every one of her messages and the gift of partaking in her journey.

"I feel safe among 8 million people. You have to keep moving, so many people. People are living an existential moment, happy with friends and selfies and life. It's real here. And down to earth. This is where I want to be. YOU DO NOT HAVE TO THINK HERE."

Having landed in the heartbeat of the WorldPride festival, Sean/a wasted no time taking in all the sights. She was her own statue of liberty, free from any sense of discrimination and oppression, having docked on the safe shores of acceptance among the masses.

Finally.

Staying at the Marriott Marquis, smack-dab in the center of everything, she couldn't deny the sense of celebrity that swirled about her as she asked a security guard to escort her to her room after trying to figure out the complicated high-rise elevator. She rose high above the flashing neon signs there in the center of trendy individualism.

Sean/a was slated to spend four days in New York City, representing intersex individuals and participating in all the WorldPride events. She sent me schedules of trans "call to action" meetings and photos of "end intersex surgery" signs. In that moment, she was living her best advocacy self, garnering attention yet sharing the spotlight with millions who had gathered in honor of respecting human differences and the right for all to live as they saw fit.

Nothing could have prepared her for the energy of New York City, but she LOVED all of it—Times Square, her room at the Marriott Marquis, being in the middle of all the action. She loved the freedom to express herself; wearing hot pink and purple in her hair barely got her a second glance in NYC. In fact, she loved it so much she wanted to move there immediately. (I had to remind her that the incessant noise and crowds, as well as the harsh winters, would be quite an adjustment from desert life; but we did take a moment entertaining the idea, looking online for apartments upon her return.)

During her visit, Sean/a felt adventurous enough to take a train upstate to White Plains to catch a WNBA game, another highlight of the journey. On the way back from that event, she messaged, "I am crying. It's all so overwhelming in the best way. I was on the train to the WNBA game, and it hit me; I am at home. It's a feeling I cannot explain."

She added some details a moment later: "I met a former WNBA player. I have been blessed with a NY bagel, a shake, burger, and pizza, and such a collection of fascinating people. Here, food is hospitality."

Although I didn't take the trip with her, I felt the gift of following along via her many text messages throughout the journey, such as when she told me, "Can I tell you again how blessed I feel at the opportunity to travel? First to San Francisco and Sacramento, and now NYC!"

Her ability to jump into the unknown with childlike enthusiasm and relish every interaction as an opportunity is such a rare gift in this day and age; it was a joy to behold.

Just as when I awaited news from the airport for her first flight to San Francisco, I had been nervous about her traveling so far. What if she got lost in the big city? What if she was overwhelmed by the crowds? I didn't need to worry. Sean/a proved herself to be extremely resourceful and didn't hesitate in asking for help and directions if needed.

"My brain wakes up with the novel stimuli and excitement of figuring my way around a new environment," she assured me, adding, "For some reason I really feel like I am home. There's peace of mind and spirit; I'm not so determined to do or be something."

I can't describe my relief at reading that, continuing to follow her slow and steady journey toward finding a place of inner peace and belonging. It both astounded me and paradoxically came as no surprise that she would find such a place—for a few days, at least—among millions in an immense and crowded city she had never been to before. Just part of the paradox that is Sean/a.

My anxiety dissipated with every enthusiastic message she sent my way. She observed, "So many people use their hands here to make things. Everyone is aligned: vocal, brash, they speak their mind. The tone of voice dictates everything."

In her synchronistic fashion, Sean/a also found a friend she knew from La Jolla in a sea of unfamiliar faces. Sean/a had become the seasoned traveler and intrepid adventurer I knew she could be. Her trips culminated in this one defining moment to be able to put the spotlight on the issue closest to her heart: intersex rights and protection.

"So much community awareness here. There is a closeness I can't explain; it's like family in my soul."

~ ~ ~

These experiences were so very fulfilling for both of us. Watching her blossom and enjoy every adventure with awe and delight was heartwarming. At times, those around me would lament the time, money, and stress spent on Sean/a … but then they would see just how wholeheartedly and enthusiastically she availed herself of every new experience. Not to mention the imprint it left on her soul and that of others.

It was so worth it! No one could contest that investing in Sean/a in this way had great humanitarian reverberations; the return on investment was unmatched in human capital. With the numerous stories she had to share, it was clear to me that the people she touched along the journey—from flight attendants to taxi drivers to people in the subway—would be forever changed, even if in a small way, by their time in the Sean/a-verse.

The realization came to me that Sean/a was able to go forth on these adventures only after creating a strong foundation of security. She was building a new platform of independence with purpose and zeal. After years without aviation, she was flying high and accomplishing so much in such a relatively short time.

Her willingness to stretch herself outside of her comfort zone ironically landed her where she was most comfortable—in a sea of humanity where she felt right at home. Sean/a was a friend of the world.

~ ~ ~

One of the most meaningful travel experiences occurred just after her birthday with a visit to her former hometown of Northglenn, Colorado.

My daughter's biological father, Aaron, had heard about Sean/a's desire to return to the town in which she had lived most of her early teen years. A former avid skier at home in the mountains, altitude sadly had become my nemesis, so Aaron graciously offered to take her around her old neighborhood. He even included a meetup with her old high school friend Steve, whom she hadn't seen in forty years.

Aaron also took Sean/a to Red Rocks, from where they Face-Timed me. I relished seeing the joyous smile on Sean/a's face as she said, "Red Rocks, this place, makes you know God exists."

Aaron then drove her to her old house, school, and church, where Sean/a marveled at how little had changed. I agree with Sean/a's compliment to Aaron that he showed courage by offering to hang out with Sean/a in a more socially conservative environment.

"I appreciate Aaron for taking me through the Denver area, but I am sure he got some flak for being around me," she observed.

Regardless of my supplying her with a fleece sweat outfit, size 15 Uggs, and Aaron giving her one of his Patagonia jackets, she still donned a sports bra with exposed mid-riff in the cold. We all had a chuckle about that. Sean/a was true to her spirit no matter where she went.

Although Sean/a still wasn't ready to be in direct contact with her sister, Robin, I mediated texts between the two of them. This gave me the unique opportunity to share in the wonderful late childhood and teen memories they had during that time. Incredulity regarding a fence near their home that hadn't been fixed in all this time. Rec-ollections of Robin's helicopter flight from the church parking lot as she went into labor. Sean/a drew comfort from the connection and validation Robin's texts provided during her visit.

The quaint Colorado town of their childhoods had been so welcoming and safe, and Sean/a relished the memories of their time as a family. She expressed gratitude to Aaron for providing her with such a wonderful reconnecting opportunity. She even did her mood-walk therapy in the snow near her hotel in downtown Denver.

Sean/a marveled at the area's new airport and sent me a text saying, "Doc, they even have an area where skis get delivered in baggage claim." Her childlike enthusiasm brought a smile to my face, how things most of us take for granted generate so much excitement.

After dropping her at the airport, Aaron exclaimed to me over the phone, "I'm a Sean/a fan. She loves life!"

Indeed, she does.

It is so inspiring how fascinated she is by local and global cultures. It gives her such joy to imagine spreading her particular blend of optimism and advocacy beyond American borders.

"Hey Sean/a, what would you think about going back to WorldPride? In 2025 it is hosted by our nation's capital in the heart of Washington, DC. Then we could head over to EuroPride in Lisbon, Portugal. Do you think you'd be up for the trip?" I was almost giddy with the thought of all that colorful energy and cross-cultural exchange.

"Doc, I can see it now, in my LGBT Hoka shoes, walking the Camino and wearing a T-shirt with our book cover on the front and 'stop intersex surgery' on the back," she laughed.

"The LGBTQIA community sure is giving me a chance to express myself in a way I thought would be impossible. This year is going to be so special! I sure hope customs is prepared for Sean/a haha."

I felt a surge of what can only be described as complete certainty that this is exactly what we had been led on the path to do all those years ago. Sean/a was always meant to be a global ambassador.

"Maybe we could hit up Pride Paris and Pride London as well? This is your year!" I told her, as I was getting more and more excited at the prospect of introducing Sean/a to some of the world's greatest cities and during such a momentous declaration of solidarity, unity, and GLOBAL community.

From a street corner stoop in La Jolla to the Portuguese Way, El Camino de Santiago, one of the most spiritually inspired walking paths in the world: Hers is a truly significant pilgrimage.

"I don't know what to say, I am overwhelmed by the blessings and opportunity to stand up for intersex rights. I have six months to plan my outfits and my wigs. This is going to be unreal; so much fun with so much purpose!" she iterated, and then reminded me, "I'm sure glad I have a translator app on my phone. In case my outfits don't speak for themselves."

She stood a foot taller as she envisioned herself at EuroPride, "I'm so honored to go to a country in which its Miss Universe representative is a beautiful Trans-woman. Portugal and the Netherlands have both sent their finest to represent them in the pageant. All due to the forward-thinking part-owner of the entire conglomeration, who is herself a MF transgendered human being. I love this new spirit of inclusion."

"How apropos. Sean/a, can you believe the theme of this year's WorldPride is the 'Fabric of Freedom' and the global call to action?" I joked with her. "Fabric, Sean/a. It says on their website that fabrics as expressive symbols communicate identities, struggle, and forms of resistance. Could this be more perfect?"

"In all seriousness, Doc, creativity and self-expression goes right to the core." She continued, "You know, one of the things I learned from my friends in the police department is how you identify your-self in public is who you are and reflects your state of mind."

And then, in a laugh-out-loud, only Sean/a could say it so per-fectly statement, she ended the conversation with, "If you are a bas-ketball player, you are not going to wear a baseball uniform."

Gotta love how her mind works. And how exactly does it work? That was for me, a psychologist, the million-dollar question.

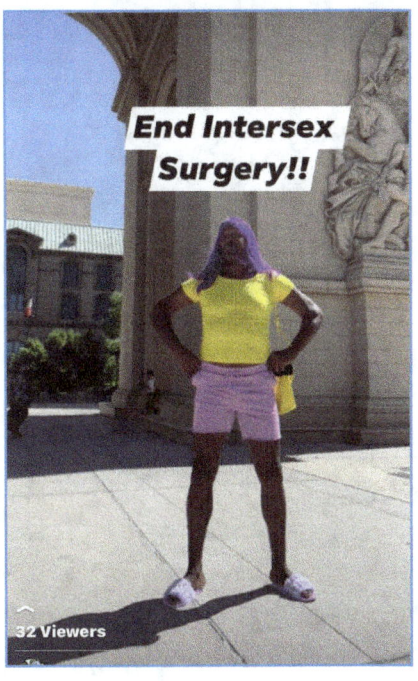

CHAPTER 10

Aspects of Mental Health

"You have to respect everyone. You may not like them or what they stand for, but you must respect them as fellow humans. I believe that everyone has a right to a nice, quality way of living. I would love to represent a philosophy or an idea that justice will prevail for everyone who has been through something challenging."

~ Sean/a

Most of the time, Sean/a lives passionately in the present. She appreciates each moment as sacred. From her long, meditative "mood-walk therapy" to honoring the sanctity of each interpersonal connection, she is a beacon of understanding and insight.

Her unyielding encouragement and support toward her communities, especially those in the LGBTQIA, are an unparalleled example of compassion. Her infectious enthusiasm and contagious spirit are pure, honest, and open, as she embraces fellow humans with unbounded joy.

Sean/a has enriched my spiritual understanding immensely, and she has my utmost admiration for the patience she shows to those who have not yet attained her level of conscious understanding. Her tireless curiosity and team mentality allow her to see each human being as part of a greater cosmic connection. In maintaining this perspective, she serves as an example to wounded hearts with her own portrayal of courage under pressure, dignity, and thriving despite circumstances.

On a daily basis, she selflessly shares her time and honors the many questions from curious (and sometimes discourteous) passersby. Sean/a responds to others even when it's inconvenient or uncomfortable for her personally.

Sean/a gleaned a unique form of wisdom from her many years as homeless and in the margins, and she imparts this to encourage paradigm shifts toward kindness and understanding. Her commitment to stand up to bullies and protect those who are being transgressed against is valiant and becomes all the more a call to action for the greater community to stand up to protect her and others who have been historically marginalized.

Sean/a has made a myriad of sacrifices in her commitment to living her truth—undaunted, fully, and with integrity. By doing so, she has the ability to enrich all who cross her path, inspiring others to fulfill their potential—if they would only take a closer look at the spiritual strength and kindness she portrays. Her determination and fortitude amidst suffering invites empathy from many around her in the community.

But not all. Why is this? Perhaps a discussion of mental health is in order.

Let's return to the fundamental questions. How do we know when we have mental health … or when we've lost it? How do we define mental health? Or mental illness? How is it, at once, defined by others and yet so utterly personal and subjective?

Arms outstretched and flailing, voice booming, hair flying everywhere, Sean/a was clearly distressed. She wore a beautiful blue dress, yet her tightly clenched grip on the purse she held indicated the level of her anguish. An inner struggle precipitated by external events.

Sean/a was often seen "talking" with internal parts of self—presumably when they would want to be witnessed or given attention. I noted her motioning them away with her hands, saying, "Guys, guys, not now." This sometimes occurred when we would meet for lunch at Smashburger or Juice Crafters when she was managing the stress of a social interaction in real life, in locations where her behavior might be more scrutinized.

I had just dropped my daughter off at a study session, and I had some time to catch up with emails. Sitting on an outside bench in downtown La Jolla, I had a front-row seat to the unfolding drama. One by one, shopkeepers heard her coming down the street and closed their doors. This wasn't their first encounter with such outbursts; some had filed complaints with the city, admonishing Sean/a as a public nuisance.

Hoping to circumvent more of such issues, I approached Sean/a calmly, cheerfully calling out, "Hey, Sean/a."

This is what I have encouraged the local community to do when encountering her in a perturbed state. I witnessed a momentary reorientation as she straightened her hair and pulled herself together; she immediately shifted into her more grounded and ladylike persona.

"Sean/a, what's going on?" I asked.

"I've had it!" she said, frustration evident in her voice. "Enough is enough. Those boys should be ashamed of themselves. Look at the state of my dress! And it smells like beer."

"What happened?" I asked, both out of concern but also to give her the chance to vent.

"I was just walking down the street, minding my business, when a car full of teenaged boys started calling me names. Probably tourists on spring break." She huffed and tried to smooth down her dress a little more. I noticed the damp patches that reeked of beer.

"They were harassing you?"

Her voice amped up. "I just kept walking along, like I always do, but they wouldn't leave me alone. Then the loudest boy threw an open beer can at me." She gesticulated wildly as she spoke, still understandably frazzled. "He almost hit me in the head!"

Sean/a was irate. Looking at her standing so tall, I knew she could've likely taken them all on, then and there, her stature alone conferring a huge advantage. But they'd remained in their vehicle and opted for a quick getaway.

Too shocked to react, too proud to cry, and all too aware of her lack of power, Sean/a opted for the next best thing, which was to angrily diffuse her pain into thin air. The problem with this approach was that some saw it as harassment. Although she had been the one harassed, with nowhere to put her extreme frustration and rage, she let it explode the only way she knew how.

Unfortunately, none of the bystanders looking on in interest or shopkeepers behind their closed doors were privy to the backstory. They only saw Sean/a's noncontextual reaction and, as people often do when they feel helpless or lack understanding, they let fear predominate. Some in the community considered Sean/a's actions at times like this a threat to their right to peaceably exist.

Sure enough, I saw a police car slowly driving down the street toward us. I'd seen it all unfold before. A similar cascade of events. The police are called, and social services are asked to intervene. I hoped it could be easily diffused this time around. Sean/a had developed a good relationship with many on the local police force over the years. She was cooperative and compliant when in her calm state.

The vehicle pulled up to the curb near us. A moment later, a couple of officers stepped out.

"Hey, Sean/a," one said. He stood near his vehicle instead of approaching. I realized he was making an attempt not to appear aggressive, and I appreciated his discernment. "Everything okay?"

"No, everything is not okay," she said, gesturing at herself. "Look at my dress."

"You want to tell us what happened?" the other officer asked.

She explained the situation again, this time in a calmer voice, though still visibly upset.

"Can you corroborate this?" one of them asked me.

"I'm sorry. I didn't actually see it unfold. But I definitely know the type of young people who do this. Probably tourists, as Sean/a mentioned."

The officer turned back to Sean/a. "Why don't we get you a coffee? We'll keep an eye out for the vehicle you described. Don't worry, all right?"

She nodded and accepted their offer, and I left her in good hands. But I was not at peace. The incident had passed, yes. Until the next injustice would take place, pushing Sean/a past her breaking point once again.

The shopkeepers who had closed their doors, as well as the general public, were rarely updated on the negative precedent or the positive outcome, so the cycle of frustration and fear continued. Some of the articles about Sean/a that had been published in the *La Jolla Light* were meant to address these communal concerns, to offer a bridge toward understanding some of the inner challenges Sean/a faced while also respecting the public's right to feel safe.

As I headed back the way I had come, I passed a women's boutique I frequented, which was owned by a wonderful woman who knew about my friendship with Sean/a. She also knew I was a trained clinical psychologist. She stepped out onto the sidewalk.

"Hey, Kirsten, everything okay?"

"Yes," I answered, shaking my head in exasperation. "Just another group of young guys who think it's great entertainment to pick on Sean/a. I don't get it."

"She was pretty upset this time," my friend observed. "I heard her passing by."

I simply nodded, not knowing what else to say.

"You know, my mother struggled with schizophrenia," she said. "I feel so bad for Sean/a because I feel like I see some similarities, you know? I empathize with her."

I thanked my friend, appreciating that not everyone jumped to negative conclusions regarding a person's struggles with mental health and dignity. A lot of people in our community really did try to understand.

It was probably time for another article in the *Light*. I hoped to educate others that Sean/a was not a threat. My goal was to turn the perception of her behavior from menacing to benign, as well as spread an awareness of how to help or even intervene if community members saw Sean/a being treated unkindly.

Sean/a's pride and strong belief in the right to authentically express herself have been pillars of strength that helped her survive unthinkably challenging times. I wanted others in the community to understand that and learn how to de-escalate a situation—not just with Sean/a but with anyone suffering momentary mental distress. One never knows who in the community at any given moment might react as Sean/a did, with even more dire consequences.

CHAPTER 10

It is imperative that one's attempt is, first, to do no harm while supporting another's inalienable rights, and second, to impart understanding and practice awareness.

~ ~ ~

A long-term mentor, friend, and pioneer in the field of Dissociative Disorders, Dr. Ralph Allison, was the first to offer up ideas of an Inner Self Helper (ISH) or spiritual ally that comes to aid a person during times of duress.[11] These ISHs appear to cross amnestic barriers and have access to the collective heart and inner wisdom of an individual. Fearful, hidden, and mistrusting aspects of a person's Self are illuminated and assuaged by this far more insightful and divinely guided aspect of one's true Essence.

As a clinician and psychologist, my inclination regarding Sean/a's behavior pointed toward dissociative schizophrenia, a rare subcategory of a trauma-induced yet biologically based disorder; however, I am loath to tie Sean/a down to any discrete disorder. Although I am a clinician, I am not HER clinician. I am her friend, and she is mine.

At the same time, in the spirit of educating, perhaps loosely tethering her to some traits that appear to overlap with this constellation of symptoms as they are uniquely expressed would help the lay person better understand the potential characteristics of such a condition.

Canadian psychiatrist and author Dr. Colin Ross first identified dissociative schizophrenia—as a subgroup of the schizophrenic population—more likely to have had significant trauma as a potential causative factor. Ross also indicated that those with this form of schizophrenia might be more responsive to psychotherapy.[12] Individuals struggling with this disorder have real hope for

11   Ralph Allison, *Minds in Many Pieces: Revealing the Spiritual Side of Multiple Personality Disorder* (CIE Publishers, 1999).
12   Colin Ross, *Dissociative Schizophrenia: A Proposed Subtype of Schizophrenia* (Wiley Online Library, 2018).

recovery based on cognitive behavioral, supportive, and educational strategies.

Returning to the scene that began this chapter, as well as numerous similar scenarios over the years, I hope that providing a grounded context eases the minds of individuals who want to hold Sean/a solely accountable for these events. At times, she may not have the agency or locus of control to choose her behaviors.

~ ~ ~

Sean/a and I have had some interesting discussions regarding what it means to be mentally healthy or not. There are some who would describe Sean/a as grandiose, delusional, narcissistic, or psychotic. Others have noted her schizophrenic or manic tendencies. Still others might give her the benefit of the doubt and say she's highly resilient, creative, and adaptive and has brought forth survival-based internal resources, emanating from a struggle beginning in childhood wherein she learned to depend upon and primarily fend for herself inwardly, calling on life-saving spiritual defenses.

Likely, all possible hypotheses have value. When placed in the context of having to live life as a "category of one," each action and reaction appears to make sense, even if only to Sean/a at times. What remains consistent, however, is the preternaturally upbeat attitude Sean/a brings to each day, ready to face whatever adversity or blessing the day brings.

In all cases, she's a harbinger of hope, a great example of post-traumatic growth.

Five years ago, I received an alarming medical diagnosis: that I had one year to live. My children were teenagers, and so many concerns and fears went through my mind during that desperate time. To say I was struggling would be a huge understatement.

Out of concern for Sean/a's long-term well-being, I told her it might be a good time to get in touch with her sister, who might need to pick up where I left off if the worst came to pass.

"Wouldn't it be wonderful if you could connect with your grand-nephews?" I asked. I broached the idea of her relocating out of state in the event that anything happened to me. She got lost in thought, appearing momentarily receptive to the idea, but we never spoke about it again.

The medical diagnosis with its gloomy prognosis turned out to be erroneous, and I was (and continue to be!) so grateful for what felt like a new lease on life. During that stretch of paralyzing uncertainty for me, Sean/a checked in and sent me positive quotes EVERY SINGLE DAY until my medical reports came back with a more fortunate prognosis. She showed up for me wholeheartedly, with presence and compassion.

I dare say that is an example of a mentally healthy, self-actualized human being.

Her openness and embracing attitude have served her well, and I am hard-pressed to imagine another who has gone through such adversity and manages to greet each new day humbly and full of vitality. Is this a mental disorder? Or should we not all aspire to find such peace in our hearts to rise above injustice and seek the light in ourselves and others?

Those with dissociative disorders often have delusional thinking and hear voices; such symptoms appear to be an internal reaction to their early environment. If we assume, as Dr. Ross proposes and I concur, that the part of the self that makes decisions "is not located in Newtonian space," but rather "exists at the quantum mechani-cal level," then a commitment to change takes place at that deeper quantum level. The process of change and/or recovery then trickles down to effect change in the conscious or "electromagnetic environment" of the brain.

This resonates with the numerous synchronicities that occur through and around Sean/a. Many clients I treated at Ross's National Treatment Center for complex trauma and dissociation exhibited similar electromagnetic brain-mind field shifts. These changes in electromagnetic energy altered the environment of the brain at the biochemical level. As a result of this research, Ross proposed that dissociative schizophrenia is "simultaneously a biological, psychological, social and spiritual problem," with therapy able to interact with and have an impact on all these levels.

The voices Sean/a reacts to at times are perhaps no more complex than her inner thoughts and emotions making the attempt to communicate with her, the goal being to integrate the voices with the other parts of her overall self. As Ross points out, those voices "are not the enemy, although they can be critical and even abusive," perhaps from longstanding trauma and loneliness. Paradoxically, an internal aggressor aims to keep the self safe even though it appears to be self-abusive.

I generally witnessed Sean/a's internal "others" presented as nothing but friendly "protectors," with her attempting to be the leader among a chorus of selves wishing to be known. In therapy or on the streets, talking to one's "inner voices" or the internalized parts of oneself is a welcoming approach. It is a practice that understands these voices have functions, meaning, and purpose—not the least of which is safety and survival.

Sean/a's holistic approach to managing her internal stress is her extensive mood-walk therapy. She walks countless miles and lets her stress out verbally. Then she goes home, eats healthily, and abstains from drugs and alcohol. The beauty of this approach is that possible negative side effects of taking medication—such as tardive dyskinesia—are minimized.

CHAPTER 10

Through my interactions with Sean/a, I have become a huge proponent of the right to choose for oneself the medication-free path to healing, leaving her brain available for post-traumatic thriving. Sean/a stands firm in her devotion to self-expression, believing at her core that she has the right to exist as she wishes. She is unapologetically genuine and true to herself in her choice to live drug- and medication-free. She allows her brain and body the freedom to retain its athletic prowess and robust health.

This is the way she chooses to approach life.

The complications of side effects for some, who worship their healthy body's full functioning as Sean/a does, are beyond what they consider a tolerable risk. This approach doesn't work for all, nor am I implying an anti-med crusade; rather, the discussion and decision is personal to each individual situation.

In Sean/a's case, having been in medical facilities and program mandates that required her to give up her personal drug-free choice in the name of medical and symptom management, Sean/a has since chosen to live life on her terms. Free from side effects. Free from anxiety about medication complications.

In addition to the general stress of living uncomfortably on the streets, Sean/a suffered one injustice after another committed against her, yet the adaptive aspects of her mental challenges—and her apparent lack of insight into their origins—have allowed her to remain calm in the face of what others might consider unacceptable uncertainty. Rather, she maintains a sense of destiny and special purpose, and an appreciation for life and her relationships, which gives her hope. Post-traumatic thriving is possible when one is aligned with a fundamental guiding Source and purposeful mission, as Sean/a clearly demonstrates.

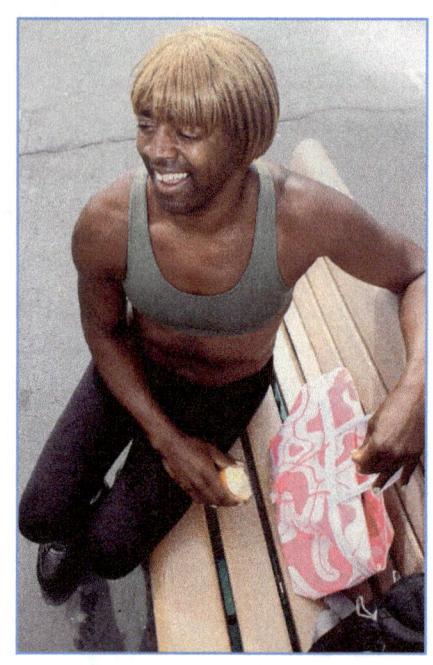

CHAPTER 11

Becoming Sean/a

"To reconnect with yourself requires spending time alone to discover who you really are and to recognize your internal conflicts, so you can graciously move past them."

~ Sean/a

"It's now or never," Sean/a told me over the phone. I heard the trembling in her voice. "I'm in the taxi. I was planning on showing up at the high school reunion as Sean, but I've changed my mind. I'm wearing white leggings and a striped top. And my purple wig, you know, the real long hair."

"I'm so proud of you," I said, caught up in her excitement and happy to hear her decision to present herself as Sean/a. "You've got this."

"I mean, I might as well be me, right?" she continued with a lively laugh. "Sean/a's debut. I'm excited! Oh, I've got to go. I think we are there already."

I might have felt almost as excited as she did, but I was also just as nervous for her. Sean/a shines with an otherworldly presence, but now she was going to be amongst those who had known her during her formative years. Sean's family had moved to Vegas for his senior year of high school, and he had immediately immersed himself in school culture.

Would those who knew her as Sean accept her as Sean/a? At the same time, I understood that it was only as her authentic self that she would be able to fully enjoy reconnecting with those she held so fondly in her memory.

Sean/a hadn't been to Las Vegas in 21 years but had been updating me regularly once she'd learned about the upcoming Las Vegas High School reunion, through a couple of group chats on social media. She had gone back and forth a dozen times on whether she should go.

"I shouldn't go," was where she started. "There are too many triggers. Like the Celine Dion song, 'It's all coming back to me now.' We could write a book on my many triggers in Las Vegas."

"Oh yeah?" I asked. "Such as?"

"Where do we start?" Sean/a laughed. "I need a couch, lol, Sin City 101."

Even though she joked about that, I assumed she wouldn't divulge much about this time in her past. Sean/a was at the same time an open book and a private person, especially when it came to some aspects of her early years.

I changed the subject. "It's funny that we were born a month apart and graduated from high school in the same year."

"But not the same high school. Otherwise, you'd be coming along too, and I wouldn't be so nervous. I mean, they all know me as who I was before."

I nodded, knowing exactly what she meant. "First, decide if you are going to go. And if you do, you'll know what to do next, Sean/a. You always do."

I had encouraged her, but now I had to wait to hear about the outcome. I hoped she wouldn't regret this step she'd taken to embrace herself by reconnecting with places and people from her past—showing up as Seana.

After a few hours of "radio silence" while she was at the reunion, the texts started pouring in. The first one read, "That was the best day of my life."

I took a deep breath, not realizing how tense I had been on her behalf, and breathed a sigh of relief. She sent me photo after photo from the evening reunion and after-party, telling me she shed a tear of joy when she was instantly embraced and recognized.

"I can't believe I almost didn't come. I talked with people I had known as a teenager, enjoyed deep conversations. Caught up on thirty-five years of memories."

It seems that Sean/a's enthusiasm piqued everyone's curiosity. No surprise there. She received her share of well-wishes for the future and has been active on the school's social media groups since. She loves being part of these networks, using every opportunity to engage her peers in lively discussions.

In fact, she had used some of her funds to contribute to her community colleges and high school, as well as to her church and various sports and other professional organizations. It was easy to see how she had become student body president and class treasurer back in the day.

I was overjoyed she had taken yet another leap of faith.

I pictured her preparing to go to her reunion dressed as Sean, and at the last minute changing her mind and bravely deciding to show up as Sean/a in all her glory. Purple wig, leggings, purse, and bejeweled flip-flops; only her energy would have glowed more than her accoutrements.

～～～

Not long after her trip, the two of us met to catch up.

"Kirst, do you remember when I used to show you my words for the week?" Sean/a asked.

"Sure, I do. You sent them to me every single day."

"Can you imagine the power of organizing people's lives if we could all just take the time to reflect? For years, I've lived by this routine."

I nodded. "I am in awe of how you've kept your routines even when you were in uncertain circumstances and had nothing permanent going on. It's inspiring."

"Well, accountability is next to forgiveness and godliness in my book. It's important." Sean/a's frequent smile appeared on her face. "We are just so blessed. I am so happy. Every day is the best day of my life."

Her enthusiasm was, as always, contagious. "Why do I feel like you say a version of that every day, Sean/a?"

"Well, we are breathing. I feel safe and I have my community. I am busy and full of hope. Clarity. And gratitude."

I couldn't argue with that.

As I write this, Sean/a has just sent a text about how much fun she has had passing out book cards at the Thursday Street Fair and how she spent an hour talking with a gay police officer friend in Palm Springs. She said it reminded her of how it felt to be accepted for who she was at the reunion.

This officer is the only openly gay officer on the force and said he had always wanted to speak with Sean/a about how she is so comfortable being true to herself, but that she was always on one of her

172

long walks and hadn't wanted to disrupt her stride. She reiterated what a blessing it was when people confided and opened up to her and how it made her feel even more connected to her community.

"We all want the same things, Doc. It's amazing. Every time I talk with someone new, I'm reminded of our shared struggles. We are never alone."

Sean/a's story feels like an unveiling at times, an unlayering and a becoming that is a story unto itself, not to be obscured by the eventual "finished" version of Sean/a. (Are any of us ever truly "finished" in our lives?) It seems an affront to Sean/a to separate her from the process of becoming, which she gracefully maneuvers daily.

When Sean/a was in the beginning stages of adjusting to life off the streets, I would get input from various members of my family regarding my attempts to get Sean/a more social services (much easier said than done) or queries as to why I needed to make more sacrifices to make sure Sean/a got her weekly money for food.

Had I fully considered the financial ramifications of taking on Sean/a's expenses over the years after that initial GoFundMe fundraiser, I doubt I would have been able to commit to the level of help we've ended up giving over the years. The journey has been taken one step, one tiny sacrifice at a time.

Yes, I received my fair share of well-deserved but well-meaning comments such as, "You took on more than you could handle." While true, through it all, we somehow never faltered in support of the original commitment to Sean/a.

My goal was that she would never have to spend another night on the streets. Check.

Those in my circle helped as they could. My family, above all, made all of this possible with their generous support of me. I always had the desire to live my life paying it forward, with the belief that "To whom much is given, of the same much is expected."

Sean/a approaches life with a similar ethic. In good times and bad, she has always felt "part of the bigger plan," as she has put it. She wouldn't hesitate to add, however, "God doesn't bless a mess. I knew God would bless me for doing the right things."

Love is at the heart of turning tragedy into triumph and strengthening one's faith.

My brother's tragic, accidental death thirty-six years ago opened my soul to a much broader community of healers, the everyday folk who had experienced post-traumatic growth through simply waking up to face each day following a complete and utter shake-up of their lives and worldview, not to mention the grueling task of mending a shattered heart.

This was true not only for me but for my parents as well during that time. It became our experience as a family. Together, we received a share of blessings through adversity. Communities of survivors and thrivers, in all walks of life, were the glue that helped us start putting the pieces back together.

When we tend to the wounds of others, we help to heal our own. My parents philanthropically touched so many as a result of shared communion through suffering and healing. Community is the antidote for the isolated elements in our wounded narrative histories. Meaning is reconstructed through one story, one right action, one hopeful gesture at a time.

As my family pressed forward, their guiding mission to not only honor my brother—whose life was so sadly cut short—but also to spread his goodwill and helpful spirit to those who were similarly walking the edge of despair was the key to healing. As grief encircles lives and clouds perceptions, compassionate communities become a lifeline.

I know, beyond a shadow of a doubt, that Sean/a's and my family's paths were perfectly constellated to interact to promote the greater good. In my decisions over the years, I am merely following my parents' and Sean/a's example that in every newfound connection and path, encountering others to buoy one's journey is a stabilizing force that has unquantifiable mutual rewards and benefits.

And so, no matter where I was in the world or what I might have personally been dealing with, I always managed to find a way to wire Sean/a her weekly funds so she could pay the bills. While doing so, I often thought about the struggles so many families face in keeping their heads above water.

I couldn't figure out why, with all the funding surplus directed toward the homeless, one single, solid, incentivized plan hadn't been arrived at. I know our current mayor of San Diego, Todd Gloria, no stranger to discrimination as a member of the LGBT community, had worked tirelessly toward a solution.

I met him in downtown San Diego once as my friend Renee (who had known him with her work through the media) and I were headed to dinner. He was surveying and interacting with the local homeless in a particularly derelict intersection and I marveled at his humanity and concern for their plight. He was truly "walking the walk."

One idea I thought might work would be a community-driven "adopt a homeless person" program, taken on by small groups of people within each local town or city, working together to help an individual and receiving funding to make those ideas materialize.

These solutions appeared self-evident to me.

I briefly spoke with a local filmmaker at a Q&A as we discussed the documentary he had made about a homeless man, "Tony" (film by the same name). He had similar thoughts when I suggested that one way to make a dent in the unhoused crisis was for small groups to rally around one homeless person and serve as mentors, help with clothing, provide jobs, etc. Most importantly, the task of such a team would be to reflect back possibilities and trust, empowering the individual to stay the course and go the distance on the difficult journey of reacclimating to society and its stressors.

To those needing more advanced therapies, it is still a much more effective and cost-saving measure to provide services and incentives to small groups who might combine their expertise to help an individual. There could then be classes and training, as well as outings such as shopping for inexpensive groceries, etc. It all sounded so simple until I watched what having been out of practice in a kitchen, for example, had done to Sean/a's ability to figure out the basics of self-care in matters like preparing a healthy meal for herself.

Any conversation about helping someone reconnect with society must include, to my mind, a human safety net. Imagine what designated groups rallying around one individual could accomplish!

~ ~ ~

As we got Sean/a housed, I also realized that although twenty texts a day might be excessive, I was literally her only support system. As overwhelming as it could be at times, I loved and cherished the opportunity to enter into useful dialogues and mentor her transition back to various aspects of life and society.

Over the years, Sean/a and I have been in almost daily communication via text or social media. This buddy system has benefited both of us as we increased our understanding of the world around us, and I believe it has been mutually rewarding. Sean/a was my apprentice as she learned vital re-adaptational skills. But I was also apprenticed by her as I learned to cope through various challenges that were outside of my hitherto more sheltered existence.

CHAPTER 11

I came to realize that, in our earlier conversations, my ofttimes for-mulaic interpretations held the danger of stifling Sean/a's free-flow-ing ideas. But I soon learned her cadence and more about how her mind operated; the soul of each interview sprang forth when our energy was aligned through a deep mutual respect.

I simply needed to sit back and let the phenomenon show itself.

As I reflected upon the nature of our many interactions together, a pattern emerged that depicted the apparently cyclical nature of spiritual striving in healing from severe trauma. In essence, trauma had pushed her to the point of desperate surrender on numerous occasions, which created an opening for the spiritual. She strived for that reconnection with the soul in her daily life—through na-ture, her mood-walk therapy, and local art she photographed on her iPhone.

Then—through conversations with others—her hope and joy permeated, and she graciously passed along the fragments of light she harnessed in a dark world as gifts. The meaning of her life is found in the richness of her daily interactions and creative expres-sions. As she passes through levels of uncertainty to assuredness re-garding who she is and her place in the world and beyond, she rel-ishes becoming part of a broader system.

Any attempts to contain Sean/a's spirit would only vanquish it. Her luminescence shines forth in every direction, and I feel graced by her presence. More than that, I feel privileged to be let into her private thoughts in addition to her very public world.

It's a paradox. There is an air of mystery surrounding Sean/a, accompanied by a twinkle in her eye that seems irresistible to most. Her dynamic personality is alive with possibility and never compla-cent. She is one among humanity who has come close to touching the Source and knowing the answers.

Yet, by the same token, she yearns to simply be a cog in the wheel, just like the rest of us. To fit in. To be useful. To be part of something.

Sean/a heralds a paradigm shift from void to meaning, and hers is a life filled with potential.

When trauma shakes a person's foundational core and the spirit becomes delocalized from its physical center in the body, the notion of an integrated "self" evaporates. In its stead, the True Self—with expanded awareness and no self-consciousness—has the potential to guide the life forward. In Sean/a's case, this life force has transcended pain, discomfort, ego, devastation, and destruction; it has risen to meet the challenges of the day with renewed faith.

This has been Sean's "hero's journey" and Sean/a's "heroine" discovery. Sean/a's trajectory represents a fundamental pattern of human experience, reflecting the psychological and spiritual growth that people move through in their lives.

One active aspect of Sean/a's calling is the challenge of creative transformation. When her original forms, assumptions, and beliefs have been challenged, she remained open to individuating and seeking her own special brand of enlightenment—which involved synchronicities and imperceptible shifts in her consciousness, propelling her ever forward.

Each of us has questions revolving around how our lives are unfolding. Are we living according to our true purpose? Have we imbued our lives with meaning? Are we resonating with the version of ourselves that we know to be authentic? Are we giving voice to those experiences that fall into the margins, which may be hard to hear or articulate?

By undertaking her quest, by following her call to adventure, Sean/a has learned to unflinchingly, unreservedly honor all of her expressions, even those that lie furthest from her comfortably constructed center.

~ ~ ~

Sean/a has developed a deep intuitive faith in her essence—her personal divinity—that doesn't require giving up rationality but rather finds a way to bridge both worlds. She knows that, from somewhere deep inside, voices emanate to direct and guide her, and she depends upon that spiritual essence to lead her.

The invisible forces opening her heart are made real by the way she experiences them, and she has developed an awareness that there is something to relate to beyond the conscious realm.

As people try to eradicate seemingly dysfunctional parts of themselves, they often send them deeper into the unconscious, where they have less control. But in that place, they also gather strength. A disturbance or distortion has an archetype at the core—a universal image, an experience—around which a personal layer can be created.

If the work of individuation involves the ego getting out of that regressive place where everything is comfortable, then clearly Sean/a manifests that journey of coming into her own psychic balance. She works to hold together disparate parts of self and connect those parts to a unifying force.

On a good day, her sparkle coupled with hearty laughter sets her apart. Her attitude of play pervades her being and creatively elicits a light from others. Sean/a's nature engages and touches the collective by creating a container for the mysterious.

As a society, there are grave consequences for marginalizing those whose voices do not echo those of the majority. It is our responsibility to let all voices be heard, but it is also to our benefit as a whole. These often-marginalized perspectives are those that might highlight truths our society and the world at large need to hear.

~ ~ ~

"I've spent so much time being by myself and being intersex," Sean/a told me once. "There aren't many people I can look to for guidance."

"Are there any sources that have helped you in your journey?"

"I've done lots of reading on the topic, but one show I absolutely love to watch is *I Am Cait*. Have you seen it?"

"I've watched a few episodes and love her humanity," I replied.

"The way Bruce/Caitlyn tackled some of her issues with such open-heartedness and the way she's so raw with her emotion and just really wants to understand … I find such beauty in that," Sean/a said. "How can someone discriminate against her when she's just trying to understand herself?"

"You probably empathize with her."

Sean/a nodded. "Definitely. I really feel her. She's just trying to feel her way through this new world. She handled adversity with grace and modeled hope as a coping skill. Hope that the world might one day come around."

We shared that same hope.

Clearly, from the way she was received at her first high school reunion, the 35th, that hope was being made manifest.

CHAPTER 12

Community and Trust

"The whole idea of life is to help others. Of course, accolades, trophies, and all of those things we achieve are important, but someone has to be really there for you. And it starts with showing up for them. Living in a supportive community is truly a blessing because I feel cared for and safe."

~ Sean/a

"**W**hy is your hair purple today?" the young girl asked. "I saw you yesterday and it was yellow," she added in a matter-of-fact voice.

I paused over my acai bowl, waiting to see how Sean/a would respond. It wasn't just adults who were drawn to Sean/a. Kids, too, were intrigued by her, and often asked questions adults wouldn't have the courage to ask.

The teacher and coach in Sean/a immediately came alive. She shone a huge smile at the girl. "I am so happy you noticed!" she answered. "Do you like the purple or the yellow better?"

"I like pink," the girl said. "But the purple is nice too."

"Why, thank you." Sean/a spoke slowly and purposefully, making direct eye contact with the girl, whose own hair was a nondescript soft brown. "It's important to dress as you feel happy and comfortable, and that goes for hair color, too."

The little girl nodded, then sauntered back to her mother, whom I noted was keeping an eye on her young daughter from where she stood in line.

Sean/a's vibrant and engaging manner entertained any and all questions, the most heartfelt and hysterical often coming from the children. I had to stifle my laughter a few weeks earlier when a boy asked her why her pink halter top made her look so "tan."

But Sean/a didn't miss a beat, answering, "Sometimes my skin gets a little darker than yours in the sun, but isn't skin amazing how it protects our bodies?"

After her interaction with the young girl, Sean/a turned back to me. "Where was I?" she asked.

"You were telling me about Kim offering to take some photos."

"Oh, right!"

As she related the event, ignoring the acai bowl in front of her for the moment, I could easily picture the sequence of events in my mind.

Laughing to herself, almost bursting with joy, the energy of her personality and pace of her stride unmistakable, Sean/a rounds the corner to the La Jolla Lamborghini dealership. She wears a slinky, bright yellow dress and a Raquel Welch-style auburn wig. She daintily yet firmly clutches a plastic purse with a beautiful floral pattern.

She greets her friend Kim with a huge hug and hello. As she speaks a million miles a minute about how excited she is to be participating in a book about her life and the lessons she has gleaned,

Kim offers, "You know I'm a freelance photographer, right? I'd love to take some photos of you around town."

Sean/a agrees with the kind of enthusiasm only she can muster. And then, with her uncanny sense of following her internal momentum, she presses on. In a flash, she waves goodbye to Kim and sets off again.

She breaks up the monotony of the endless and somewhat predictable rat race as she goes about town. Sean/a walks past the local car wash, getting a few whistles from the workers when she says, "Hey, guys," with a wave.

"Those guys at the car wash are too much," I told her, pausing her narrative. "They're still whistling at you?"

"Nah, they're just being themselves," she defended them. She must have noticed my disbelieving expression, as she added, "They have known me since my shopping cart days. Yeah, it started out as jokes, maybe even a bit of harassment, but it has turned into something else."

"Into what?" I pressed.

She tilted her head, her curls bouncing. "Into a mutual 'I see and respect you' moment as I do my day and they do theirs."

"You've come a long way from those 'shopping cart' days," I observed, remembering the time she was cited, fined 200 dollars, and summoned for possession of said shopping cart.

She'd probably passed that car wash a dozen or more times a day, running countless errands—dropping off her belongings for daily storage at a now defunct gas station, chatting with customers there, then loading her cart with resale items for local businesses. She would make a stop at Goodwill, do a coffee run, a bank run, and then jaunt over to the rec center to shoot a few hoops. Local men, women, teens, and children would join her or just look on in awe at her perfect form while on the courts.

Then she'd stop for a few hours at her local corner, sitting curbside and watching the endless parade of frenetic humanity: doctors heading to the hospital or on lunch break, moms taking their kids to jujitsu class, women in leggings headed to yoga followed by dairy-free smoothies with gluten-free granola, the ladies-who-lunch crowd, high schoolers congregating after school for shakes and Boba teas, tennis players, and moms who didn't know whether to encourage or discourage their kids' fascination with Sean/a.

Sean/a turned community at large into a character in her life's novel. She saw it in some ways as an energy, an interconnected living entity, intertwined individuals with immense power to shape the direction of our lives.

"So many people showed up for you during the Shelter for Shauna campaign," I reminisced. "It was remarkable."

"I think a lot of them chose to help because they knew I wasn't your typical homeless person. I don't drink, I don't do drugs, no felonies, no DUIs. I have friends who took care of me and said, 'We're going to help. It's our turn to step up to the plate.'" Sean/a concluded, "And so, here I am. I love my friends and my community."

Acceptance is reciprocal, with ongoing mutual benefits for its participants. We all deserve the right to be part of society; even those who apparently opt out are still a part of the greater archetype of community. The construct of healing as a whole is the only approach that makes sense here. We build community together, and we are only as strong as our weakest link.

Everyone besides Sean/a seemed to have a place to hurry off to. Yet somehow, all the while Sean/a was the only one who—in her inaction—was actually following her purpose through her presence.

Sean/a's childhood may have been fraught with insecurity, but Sean/a was indubitably attached to her community. The disruption of her early attachment bonds was supplanted by an innocent trust in humanity at large, and a coherent confidence in the too-numerous-to-count, good-hearted people of the communities in which she thrives.

Her authentic manner of relating to people during her daily routines fostered solid relationships with virtual strangers, with whom she shared mutual interests and engagement. Even when she was homeless (albeit clandestinely so), tourists who visited La Jolla annually from around the globe would seek Sean/a out to take her for coffee and reignite lively discussions that were years in the making.

Sean/a's ability to connect with all sorts of people was apparent every time we met and everywhere we went. This connection with, attention to, and genuine love of community was Sean/a's oxygen. At once personal and supra-personal, these interactions offered nourishment to the souls of all touched by the encounters—Sean/a's soul no less than the rest. Even the lady working behind the counter making smoothies wore a smile whenever Sean/a bounced into the cozy little place we frequented.

She left her mark wherever she went—a statement proven by events such as one of her collegiate teammates reaching out to offer some help with rent after learning of Sean/a's plight through the school's alumni newspaper.

Interestingly, Sean/a's attachment to community stands in stark contrast with her personal life of being without a significant other. Sean/a's pervasive self-reliance in adulthood enabled her survival on the streets and helped her develop an easy comfort with being alone. Although she enjoys being cared for (don't we all?), Sean/a has told me she is perfectly happy living by herself because she feels she is never truly alone. This comfort level doesn't preclude the longing, at times, for someone to share her life with, but Sean/a is content.

Over the years, she earned the respect of many curious individuals with her keen intellect, sharp memory, and fascinating insights into the world at large. The integrations of multiple conversations throughout each day contributed to her inner resilience. Together, the positive interactions and her astute observations helped her navigate the daily challenges of being unhoused with resourcefulness and a deeper sense of what community really is all about.

Never once have I heard Sean/a display bitterness, resentment, or self-pity. She is truly remarkable in her positivity. At one point we went to lunch at Smashburger with an individual who had heard about her story and confessed he was inspired by Sean/a's optimism regardless of her daily suffering. This individual had struggled for years with depression and was exceedingly curious regarding Sean/a's preternaturally optimistic mental outlook.

This interaction revealed to me the ways in which her creative adaptation to out-of-the-ordinary experiences could be a possible panacea for those paralyzed with anxiety and dysthymia.

"You know, you've made an amazing difference in a lot of people's lives just by being you," I said as Sean/a turned her attention to the acai bowl in front of her.

"I can't take all the credit," Sean/a responded. "I would love to give thanks to everyone who has helped so much—the community of La Jolla and people all over the world who stop and pray for others—dealing with what they are going through and still helping those who are suffering. It's all about hope and faith."

"You really have a gift of hope, you know that?" The myriad obstacles Sean/a faced daily while homeless (and the continuing challenges she faces as intersex) couldn't deter her from propelling her life forward.

"Everyone has a gift, and we must acknowledge that. For example, within a church or governing body, some people have the gift of administration. They can delegate. They are in charge. That's a gift."

"Is this something you learned from the Bible?" I asked, smiling.

"Well, it's true. There are folks who have the gift of helping; others have the gift of hospitality." She paused with a smile on her face. "I love that one. That's the people of La Jolla."

"I never really thought of it that way, but you make a good point."

"There's the gift of encouragement or exhortation. And some people love everyone and will do whatever they can to help a stranger."

"A lot of those can apply to the community of La Jolla," I said.

"You bet, Doc."

~ ~ ~

Each year Sean/a chooses a guiding word. As she struggled through her first year from homeless to housed, she chose the word trust.

Trust that the bond of friendship we had and my promise to arrange for and help with her rent and food, phone, and utilities (even when I was completely unsure where that money would come from) would be honored.

Trust that she could emerge from the mentality that she was dependent on the next interaction with one or another member of the community to secure the most basic items for survival.

Trust that she didn't need to stand in the demoralizing space of suffering countless indignities from other homeless people while awaiting a lunch handout. (Some of them ridiculed Sean/a for her manner of dress or general countenance.) This daily occurrence was made worse by the fact that they were in the same position in society, yet Sean/a retained a sense of being greater than her circumstances.

Through trust, Sean/a was starting to shed the burdens of homelessness one thought, one painstaking emotion at a time.

I used to provide her with a mani/pedi once in a while as a celebratory treat, and the staff clamored to be the ones to wait on her … literally, hand and foot. She was adored as she expressed such glee at her colorful, feminine accoutrements capped off with shiny purple, bright red, or green polish. She was fully appreciative of the services that were bestowed upon her at the time in her life when she regularly offered her services to others for pennies, quite literally.

Some in the community shared with me that, no matter what they struggled with at any particular moment, seeing Sean/a's smiles made their troubles disappear. In recognizing their shared humanity with Sean/a, folks were able to put their problems into perspective. As such, Sean/a took people out of themselves and their lives for a moment, giving them a glimpse of joy, awe, wonder and compassion, and fun.

The cooks at local restaurants often had a hot breakfast ready for her in the morning; I am so grateful that the right people always "seemed" to show up at the right time to offer a helping hand in Sean/a's life. One restaurant employee, in his strong accent told me, "Everybody loving this guy," referring to Sean (even when she was already presenting as Seana).

It's true, (mostly) everyone loves Sean/a. In return for the manager's kindness, Sean/a would stick around to offer her services in whatever fashion the manager saw fit for that day. Yes, the community fed Sean/a, but Sean/a definitely fed the community in return.

Sean/a was a public figure out of survival, not by choice. She is intersex, African American, athletic, six feet five and political (without even trying) because of her confidence in her beliefs. Her courage in buffering the high level of daily scrutiny she endured simply for being herself would be enough to drive the sanest people off the edge. But she learned to make lemonade from the sourest lemons by adding the sweetest sugar.

Those who considered Sean/a to be self-serving or even exploitative simply failed to grasp her inherent goodness. We all have a self-preservative instinct, and hers tried, at every turn, to find respite in the crowds ... scanning the sea of strangers for a compassionate soul who might offer a kind glance or comforting words of hope. Sadly, this approach was often misinterpreted.

Often, Sean/a provided philosophical guidance or spiritual direction in return for those who would reach out to her in some way, far exceeding anyone's stereotypical expectation. In my experience, when I am fully open to the realm of possibility, I feel Sean/a's positive energy to be magical, contagious, and inspiring. It uplifts me and carries my day forward. I know I am in the presence of an old, wise soul. She engages philosophically in a manner reminiscent of the gurus and sages ... an eccentric shaman with street smarts.

Undoubtedly, getting to know Sean/a is a deep exploration into the self, the mind of the universe, the soul, the heart of compassion, and the mysteries and complexities that elude yet challenge and beckon us all.

If this is mental illness, I find myself hard-pressed to deny its adaptive and palliative value. She offers a balm in a largely disconnected and cold, ego-driven world. Sean/a forces people to examine their values and core beliefs, challenge their stereotypes, and—if they are open to it—search deeply for answers that aren't always readily available or easy to bear.

For many in our greater community, Sean/a offered a license to be oneself. Whether regarding sexual orientation, creativity, or artistic expression of her colorful Goodwill outfits (herself the greatest GOOD-WILL ambassador), Sean/a deeply inspires. Designers and artists commented on her use of color and fashion, while the elderly were amused by her seeming shucking of convention … many of them having lived beyond the constraints of society in creative, artistic, scientific, free-spirited communities, and having come out the other side laughing.

Sean/a lives fully the philosophical tenet that, despite appearances to the contrary, no man or woman is an island. She honors the idea that deeply believing in one another is key to growth in our communities, yet she also realizes the power of fully believing in oneself as paramount. A strong sense of self is the springboard to living a balanced life.

She refuses to take personally the actions of a few misaligned individuals. Instead, she lets the goodness of life, her faith, and the collective energy of trust in the right people carry her forward. A walking Zen master, a true phenomenologist, Sean/a goes with the flow of what each moment presents. She wholeheartedly releases control and ecstatically lets the universe guide her.

～～～

In my doctoral research, I was blessed to interview many near-death experiencers through the years who unanimously state that our overarching purpose on earth is to love. Sean/a's success is measured in the quality of her capacity to love. Every time I saw her interacting with others—from the curious child at the restaurant to the men outside the car wash—I realized that capacity is endless.

Seana's unconditional love of humanity, her quest for truth and enlightenment regarding the human condition, her transcendence of suffering—these all serve as a stellar example, encouraging us to break free of long-held beliefs and patterns of relating that aren't in the service of growth.

The purity and transparency of how Sean/a lives her life is my definition of freedom. Her insatiable desire for joy uplifts one person at a time. She has worked to free herself from internal oppression and judgment and liberate her soul from the bondage of internal persecution and sabotage. In doing so, she is reclaiming her power and honoring her soul's destiny.

Nothing stands in the way of Sean/a's focused vision as she fully opens her being to free-flowing love, support, and wisdom. She lives in harmonic balance and manifests her ideal life in the most minute interactions. She finds true soul inspiration and playfulness while connecting with her larger purpose of spreading joy.

Bouncing along, Sean/a was on a literal daily happiness mission: Resonantly building community one trusting, brave step at a time.

CHAPTER 13

Mood-Walk Therapy

"Mood-walk therapy is everything to me. I taught aerobics in college, so I use that knowledge to help move into healing from my past. It's great time management, too. In La Jolla, the San Diego Police Department used me as their homeless outreach, eyes and ears, because I covered so much ground on foot."

- Sean/a

Confident. Bold. Gleeful. Athletic. Purposeful.

These were the words that came to my mind. Sean/a sported a neon-colored sports bra, leggings, and flip-flops as she excitedly gathered the four of us together—women with little in common except that we opted in for her walking group. As one of them, I was thrilled to be a part of what she dubbed Sean/a's Walking Club.

"People ask me why I spend so much time walking daily," Sean/a said to the four of us standing in a loose half circle around her. "Walking is my therapy. My 'mood-walk therapy.'"

Walking has been her outlet for decades; before that, she did high-impact aerobics and played basketball and tennis for stress relief. Sean/a has long touted the benefits of exercise, sunshine, and letting off steam. She was clearly all the better for her mood-walks—fitter, happier, and more connected to people and her community—and wanted to invite others to join in this part of her grand adventure.

"We all have mental distress at times to one degree or another. With mood-walk therapy, I get it out," she added.

Our small group consisted of one British tourist who visits Sean/a every year, two locals who seem to have known Sean/a forever, and me. I noticed the diversity of our little group and reflected a moment on Sean/a's keen ability to bring together people from all walks of life. But I didn't have much time for reverie. She was ready to move!

"You might think you're in shape," she started animatedly, "but let's talk about the importance of us stretching our hip flexor muscles as females. This is very important before we get started."

We dutifully followed her instructions on stretching, and then off we went. Sean/a took us on side streets and back alleys, through parks and neighborhoods, all the while filling us in on the activities she noticed from her daily wanderings about town.

"Five kids live in that house." She gestured toward the cottage-style home we passed. "They're a delightful bunch sometimes, but boy do they play noisily!"

Half a block down, she informed us, "That house has police interference. A lot!" She shook her head and kept up her purposeful stride. I considered myself somewhat fit, but was in awe of how Sean/a managed this kind of pace on a daily basis and has done so for years on end.

She paused in front of a white stucco building. "This place was built in 1945. It used to be the seat of great psychology sessions.

Even the great Carl Rogers practiced here. Great humanitarian, what warmth." Seana's depth and breadth of knowledge fascinated me.

We found ourselves on a street with several shops. "That coffee shop has the best blends. If you haven't tried it, you should stop by sometime this week. But not today! No, we're on a mission." A moment later, she paused in front of a small Mexican restaurant. "Oh, have you tasted those tacos? Yum!"

We continued into a park. There were fewer stories about the place, but she barely paused in her narrative, infusing her conversation with insights on how we should breathe. "I am so glad you joined me, ladies." She lifted her arms toward the sky and stopped for a moment, taking a deep breath. "Do you realize how great this walk is for our physical and mental health?"

Even the quieter women in our small group were laughing before long and freely participating in her stories and energy, asking questions, and actively listening.

"Sean/a," the British woman asked, "Perhaps my question is an obvious one, but I am curious as to your transition to living as Sean/a as opposed to Sean. I remember meeting you years ago as Sean. What differences have you noted in your daily life?"

I was somewhat surprised at the candid question, spoken with an impeccable accent, but this woman had not seen Sean/a since her last visit a year or more ago, so it was understandable. The difference she noticed since their last interaction must have been quite apparent.

"I think Seana is happy because she is free," Sean/a responded after a brief pause. "Sean was happy, too, but I think Sean was happy because I knew I was going to find myself someday. I used to be afraid to love life and fully embrace the idea. But now I love life and I love me."

As she explained herself in this way, I pictured that life Sean lived in the '80s—exuberantly teaching high-impact aerobics on a large stage in Pacific Beach. Perhaps it was really Seana just waiting for her debut.

"There's more to life than how you are being defined," she added. "We are all on earth for a reason, and there are always role models who have persevered."

The most apparent thing to me as we walked was how her energy (not just the fact that walking across the whole state seemed easy for her uber-fit self) was contagious. It sparkled all over us like little bubbles.

"The whole point of why we are here is to know that one person simply cannot do this alone," she added. "It has to be a unit, a core group of people. This is the fundamental lesson I learned living on the streets: the community sustained me, and I did my part to sustain it in return."

In her lived experience as a PE teacher and men's basketball player, she learned to work in coherence, not create rifts. Sean/a told me once that she was known by her friends as a nice person who never fought, and always sought harmony and solutions. In her more recent mission as an anti-bullying advocate and crusader, she carried the same desire—that people would hear this message loudly and clearly: they are never alone.

Never ever alone.

"Mood-walk therapy isn't just for one day every now and again," Sean/a told us. "I have a whole mood-walk calendar, and it goes like this: Sunday for family, Monday for work and leisure, Tuesday for gospel hour, Wednesday is fun day, Thursday is for knowledge, Friday friends, and Saturday self-love."

I made a mental note to ask her more about this mood-walk therapy calendar and what it looks like practically. For the moment, I was simply impressed at how intentional her focus was as she walked her daily half-marathon.

By the end of our mood-walk therapy, I didn't feel exhausted (despite trekking five miles). By the expressions on the faces of my companions, I think they felt the same: rejuvenated and refreshed, more in touch with our community, more connected to each other and to life. In fact, I felt absolutely buoyant—as if Sean/a's aura merged with ours and lifted us into another realm.

That interdimensional quality, along with her very grounded physicality, was purely sublime. We became a tangible part of mood-walk therapy. We felt its power, this wonderfully healing creation, Sean/a-style.

"You might know that I have key words to help me in my walking meditation," she said as our walk found us having gone full circle. "It calms the chaos. Well, before you all head back to your homes, I want to leave each of you with a word for the week."

She gave each of the women their word, ending with me.

"Kirsten, your word for the week is joy."

Not for the first time, I wondered what the community might become if they would let Sean/a be the Pied Piper of Possibility! At one point, I came close to lobbying the local schools to enlist her as a PE teacher, convinced that any conflicts in the classroom would evaporate after an hour and a half with La Jolla's finest.

Once she found security in her living situation, Sean/a was motivated to pick up where she had left off as a licensed California PE teacher and basketball coach, yet she was hesitant to attempt to take on such a vocation, which was reminiscent of the hectic lifestyle that brought Sean to a screeching halt so many years ago. But she sure could inspire!

As with many other things having to do with Sean/a, there are complexities about her mood-walk therapy. At times, chaos and havoc encroached on her life when she was misunderstood, and things snowballed from there. One reason for her extended walks—averaging around THIRTEEN miles a day in sometimes ill-fitting sandals—was to relieve stress, sometimes by verbally shouting things that needed to be released. At times, these loud angry-sounding outbursts frightened those around her, and they scurried for cover.

Thankfully, as has been the case so many times with those who encountered Sean/a, the police officers assigned to Sean/a as part of the Homeless Outreach Team made a huge difference in helping her understand both her rights and the limits to her rights. Even before I came along, she had already made allies and friends with many of the police officers. They found a way to put her endless walks to good use. In fact, they'd helped her obtain identification cards and had also directed her toward medical check-ups and psychological services at the San Diego Gay and Lesbian Center (whose staff first helped her understand and process her intersex condition).

For the most part, they understood Sean/a was trying to peacefully coexist within the community and advocated for larger discussions about homelessness and mental illness. They also played a part in helping the community understand there was no need to avoid Sean/a, much less run in fear from her, but instead to give her space and respond in a non-escalating, compassionate manner.

Once people truly understood the innocent nature of Sean/a, as opposed to viewing her as a street hustler or a menace, they were all too willing to give assistance. At night, she even helped the SDPD patrol the "beat" on her two feet.

When Sean/a struggled, the staff at the local CVS also rallied around her, understanding that she had the best intentions. Since they were one of the local businesses open the latest at night, Sean/a often lingered inside for warmth and safety. The staff came to her defense on numerous occasions.

Again, this went both ways. Their understanding of Sean/a's challenges in the proper context helped her live with dignity, but she also did her part in protecting or watching over the community on her nightly walks and keeping the cashiers company as they worked the late shift.

~ ~ ~

As the other women in our little group got ready to take their leave, Sean/a offered us one last bit of counsel.

"Keep your head up. Keep your faith." She looked at each of us in turn. "Know you are never alone; there is always someone going through something similar. It is important in life to just keep moving. Don't listen to the dream killers."

The other women thanked her and said their goodbyes. Soon, it was just the two of us.

"I can't believe I just walked five miles. It felt like just a few minutes," I told her.

"It was just a few minutes," she said with a smile.

"If you can make walking a fun activity, you can do anything," I joked.

"I'm just getting started, another eight miles to go for me today." She did a couple of side lunges. "Life's a grand adventure, Doc."

"You sure make it that way." I did a couple of shoulder rolls and checked my phone. I had a few minutes before I needed to pick up my daughter from practice. "Do you often think about how much adversity you've overcome?"

She took a deep breath. "I can't say that I think about it too often. Rebounding from adversity involves surrounding yourself with people who can help support you, people who remind you of your own strength."

"So, that's the secret?" I asked. "Having the right people in your life? I think you aren't giving yourself enough credit."

She shrugged. "I also choose to forgive and let go of transgressions against me. Many people have no idea what it's like to be harassed daily and to have one's civil liberties continually under attack."

"I can't imagine some of the things you've gone through," I affirmed.

"But through it, I've learned to try and be a calm voice of reason and actively seek out help from police officers or advocates when needed."

"You're talking about the officers on the Homeless Outreach Team?" I clarified.

"Them and so many others. When I look at my new California ID, I feel like a real person with a real address. My dignity has been restored. I never dared to imagine it, but it happened."

I was swept up in her enthusiasm as she continued, "When I look back at my life and everything that has happened, one common thread is that I've always tried to enjoy life even through the obstacles and hurdles. That wasn't easy."

"So, how did you manage to do it?" I asked.

"It's a mindset. It's all about acceptance. If I could teach a course on social intelligence, the key word would be acceptance. I finally feel legit and accepted; the future is bright, I have so much joy in my heart."

"Joy." I smiled. "That's the word you gave me for the week."

"Mine is direction." She breathed out a contented sigh. "I have so much self-direction now; I like the path I am taking. And speaking of paths, I'm off to finish my walk."

Off she went, with direction, joy, acceptance, and resilience. It was as though the freedom of movement she enjoyed during her walks fueled her capacity for resilience and gave her the mental strength to rebound from adversity. Walking served as a sort of mental housecleaning, enabling Sean/a to glean wisdom from adversity, crystallize truths, and amplify her values.

This connection with the inner self via tangible engagement with the present was one of the most remarkable benefits of Sean/a's mood-walk therapy.

Interestingly, Sean/a wasn't always on the go. By stark contrast, she could also be found sitting quietly, almost motionless, for hours outside of Verizon. This was a spot she frequented for hours on end during her years unhoused.

I was curious about this. Was sitting and staring into space her internal respite from feeling "on" all the time? Were they the so-called "negative" symptoms of schizophrenia?[13] Was it merely boredom?

It was notable to me how this bubble of mental safety she created could be burst quickly by a friendly, engaged, "Hi Sean/a," or by her suddenly getting up and walking briskly—all over town. The seemingly low-energy persona was often transformed with the gift of acknowledgment—a greeting from another person—and a lively interaction would often then ensue.

She was high-energy, full-speed-ahead or completely sedentary. There was no in-between. I think the only time I've ever seen Sean/a lower in energy—and still far above the baseline—was when she had a cold. While some might consider her high energy as hypomanic symptoms, I think they can conversely be viewed as indicative of a person who has risen above.

Sean/a has simply chosen to live unencumbered by life's stressors as her preferred mental state. Her exuberance fosters joy and connection (which was noticeably evident as I took part in her mood-walk therapy group). Her attitude conveys profound adaptational survival value.

Her hearty laugh and bold persona are not only signs of internal happiness but likely also hark back to her childhood, with observations of her brother and the culture of Vegas showgirls being flamboyant. In essence, "It's showtime" every minute of every day for her, like it or not. Thankfully, she revels in it and has touched the lives of many by being open to any and all experiences.

---

13 Negative symptoms of schizophrenia refer to a cluster of symptoms such as decreased experience of pleasure, reduced desire to have social contact, decreased speech, flattening of expression, stupor and catatonia.

Cross-culturally, Sean/a's flair is reminiscent of the colorful pageantry of Carnival in places like Trinidad and Rio—the people's unself-conscious expression of jubilation coupled with celebration. It is as if Sean/a is in a perpetual dress rehearsal and the excitement she exudes is palpable. Her performances are as genuine as one could imagine. She is always ready for her close-up.

Mood-walk therapy is the panacea for all forms of stress in Sean/a's life; it instantly calms her internal storms and eases her anguish, making her feel great and staving off discomfort. It's no wonder she loves sharing the power of that healing with the community she adores. Walking those great distances triggers a rush of endorphins, which biologically cultivates her optimism bias.

Sean/a has an incredible memory, remembering keen details of her life, people, and events. Perhaps the warmth, friendliness, and evocation of trust that Sean/a cultivates daily through her active lifestyle and community-building efforts have recalibrated and restructured her brain from its early traumatic experiences.

Her peak fitness and emphasis on nutrition have also kept the doctors at bay. Her use of fitness apps and technology to record every step motivates her to keep on track, constantly challenging and coaching herself. While on the go, she checks in with many online groups and churches, and stays connected with various well-being, fitness, and mental health chats. Her good character and mental capacity appear to have expanded and grown enhanced over the years.

During one of our many meetups, a father-daughter tennis team approached, and the father asked Sean/a, "Where do you get your happiness?"

I don't recall what she told them, but afterward she said to me, "I am asked that frequently and I stand tall. I really can't pinpoint why I'm so happy, but as the years go on, I find myself happier and happier. My joy comes from my spiritual gift of FAITH, believing without seeing. It's carried me this far and there ain't no stopping us now!"

"Was there a time in your past that you remember being unhappy?" I asked.

"I've always tried to be happy, even back then as Sean. I just didn't know how to be me. Now I am happy and me."

I noticed that she didn't exactly answer my question. Instead of focusing on the unhappy times, which I know were plentiful in her life, she chose to focus on the joy. That was part of her secret.

"I believe in life," she continued. "I believe in living. Being a cheerful giver, doing it from the heart."

By showing up exactly as she is in every moment—even while she is continuing her inner journey toward wholeness and belonging—she gives others permission to do the same. Sean/a has the audacity to be fearless and walk her way through life without constraint. Surely, this is a manifestation of joy.

As I stroll through life and its accordant challenges and triumphs, I want to maintain a component of Sean/a's mood-walk tutelage in all that I do—to feel the joy that she shared with me not just for the week but far beyond, even if I don't walk half-marathons on a daily basis like she does!

"Oops, gotta go. My app is telling me to get moving. I've completed over 700 days out of 1,000 on my daily move goal. See ya, Doc."

"Enjoy your walk. You literally amaze me, Sean/a," I stated joyously.

Congruent with Blue Zone research on the importance of nutrition, fitness, and social connection, purpose, and meaning, I believe Sean/a is on her way to outliving us all.[14]

---

14 Blue Zone research by Dan Buettner is a study of the lifestyle factors that contribute to long life and low rates of chronic disease in specific regions of the world. Interestingly, La Jolla has been posited as a future Blue Zone site of interest by the town council due to its lifestyle factors in alignment with Blue Zone principles such as focus on outdoor activities, healthy diet, and strong community ties with many centenarians.

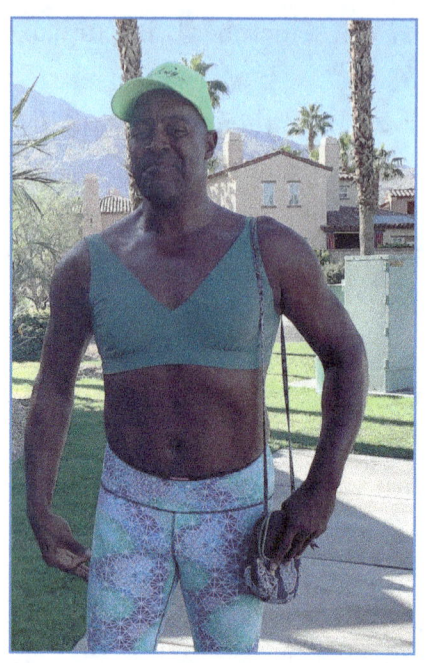

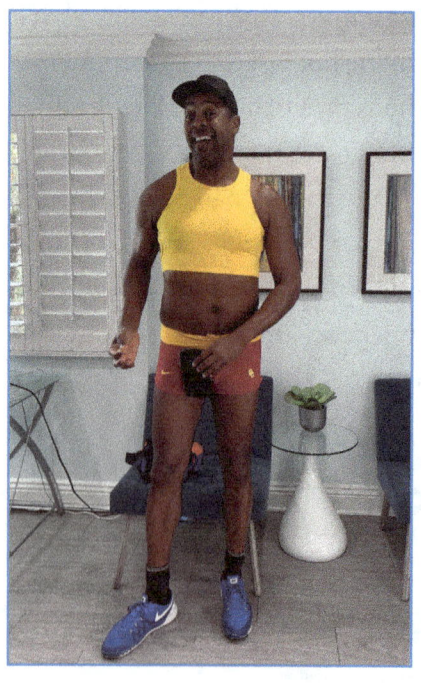

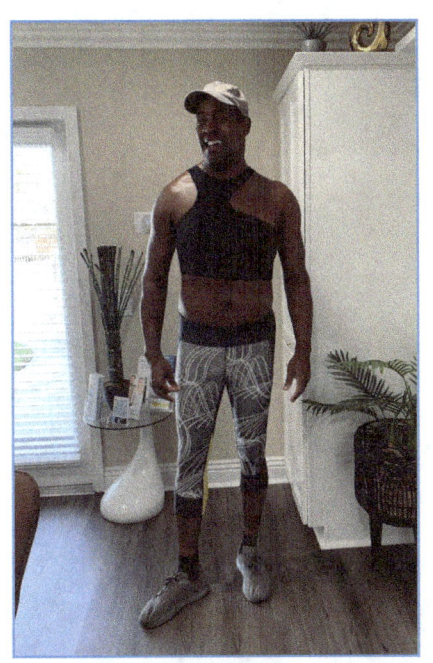

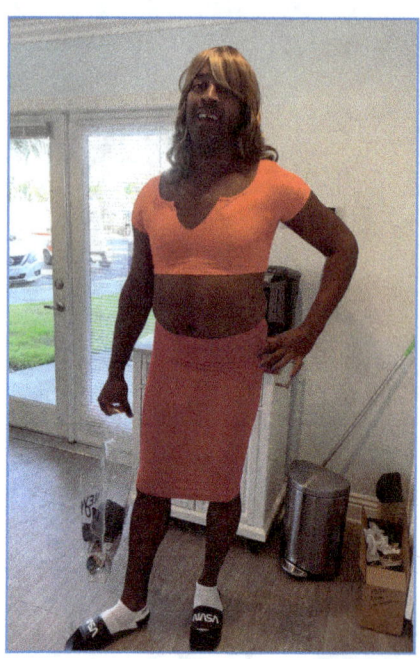

CHAPTER 14

At Home in the Desert

"Believing in myself comes from being determined that I'm going to be happy. It comes from determination that I'm going to work for something and stand for what I believe in. I don't expect everyone to be fond of who I am. There are so many boundaries we have in our world, but we need to surround ourselves with people who respect us."

~ Sean/a

While things were going well overall, I sensed the stress that Sean/a sometimes felt. There seemed to be unspoken triggers in the community from eight years of homelessness that impinged on her sense of wellness at times. Although she had a place to call home, a comfortable apartment to return to every night and rest her head, Sean/a wondered aloud to me whether there might be a place where she could feel more at ease as she rebuilt her sense of self.

She had lived in many locations in her life up to this point. Sean/a had known the vibrant city life of Las Vegas and the calmer, small-town feel during her early years in Colorado and Maryland. She had attended college in Wyoming and California. Although San Diego had been her home for three decades, there were times she voiced an interest in finding a home where the pace was slower, the people less harried, and the general stress level less intense.

I empathized with this struggle, which might have had as much to do with an inner sense of belonging as it had to do with the outside world. La Jolla had been a gracious community that offered her space to grow—from Sean to Sean/a—and embrace a fuller part of who she was. It had been a community that showed up as generous and compassionate while she was homeless, and manifested great generosity in our efforts to find housing for her.

But Sean/a was constantly seeking spaces for more growth—both outwardly and inwardly. Perhaps this town, with reminders of how things had been, was no longer the place for it. For now.

Sean/a loved the ambitious energy of La Jolla, its enthusiastic pace and intelligent people. She told me time and again how she appreciated the intellectual curiosity of the well-educated and accomplished people from around the world. (Many such folks gravitated to the jewel of San Diego due to its world-class research institutions.)

Her conversations with all kinds of people as she walked around town were stimulating and absorbing. The milieu influenced her daily interactions, and she tended to be quite visible as an eccentric member of the LGBTQIA community. I believe there were times she felt put on display, just a little too obvious. Perhaps she also sensed lingering expectations to show up in a certain way rather than have the freedom to just be herself—whatever way that self chose to manifest on any given day.

I told her once there were times in my life when I just went along with the "ditzy blonde" stereotype rather than explain that I had a master's in biomedical sciences and a PhD. Her answer was "Welcome to my daily life." She was often tragically underestimated.

With her keen ability to access other places via the internet, Sean/a grew aware of cities and towns known for their forward thinking as well as their tolerance on issues such as gender ambiguity. One result of Sean/a's involvement in online communities was that she decided she wanted to move somewhere where LGBTQIA concerns pervaded.

She started researching far and wide. While there were plenty of places to choose from, one of the locations she had always envisioned as most interesting and well-suited to her preferences was Palm Springs. Sean/a was thrilled to learn that the entire city board and council was not only gay-aware, but that the mayor-elect was a trans woman, the first in the nation. It also excited her to think of herself as a part of Old Hollywood and retiring to the desert.

We talked about this possibility at length. Moving would be a big change—and from a beachside town to the desert! It would be a drive of more than two hours from La Jolla and the life she had known for most of her adult years. But the more she considered it, the surer she became of this next step.

Sean/a was moving to Palm Springs.

We found an apartment managed by a member of the LGBTQIA community. DeWayne was an incredibly compassionate, understanding human who from the start was fully supportive of Sean/a and however he/she decided to express him/herself.

Sean/a's good friend Martina, who owned Martina's Transportation and had previously taken an interest in her situation, helped out as a taxi driver for her from time to time. Martina was all too happy to assist her move to Palm Springs and coordinated the help of her son and his friends to get Sean/a situated.

Upon Sean/a's relocation, DeWayne was patient and welcoming and helped Sean/a navigate some difficult situations with new neighbors. He kept me informed of some of the struggles Sean/a faced living in a huge apartment complex with many rules and (unruly, at times) party folks, etc. He helped facilitate new friendships and provided insights, teaching Sean/a about the lay of the land.

DeWayne soon became a cherished friend who deeply cared about Sean/a's well-being and mental health.

"Doc," she texted not long after moving, "the people of my neighborhood are so friendly, from my new friend Kim, a creative photographic artist, to the Palm Springs policewoman who saw me walking and gave me a ride to Ralph's market. It was a triple-digit day; she was so nice to do that."

I was relieved when I read that message. Although I knew DeWayne was in her corner, I had felt some concern at how the general population might react to this larger-than-life character suddenly showing up in their midst.

Sean/a texted often, keeping me updated even though we no longer lived in the same city, making interesting notes about the community's daily rhythms and other observations. Overall, she was overwhelmed by the friendliness of the laid-back Palm Springs community.

By relocating to that one-bedroom apartment in Palm Springs, Sean/a was continuing to remove the shackles of her past. It had been her choice to make this move. Nothing made me happier than knowing she was taking yet another step to embrace her freedom to live and choose as she wished.

A Wells Fargo manager who had worked with us in La Jolla said he was so impressed, remarking that Sean/a had spoken for years about one day wishing to retire to the desert, and she was actually brave and adventurous enough to do it.

His comment reminded me that Sean/a and I made a good team. When Sean/a brought an idea to me, I listened and executed. And when I brought an idea to Sean/a, she did the same.

⁓ ⁓ ⁓

"Doc, what should I bring? I am so excited. They are such gracious hosts."

I read the text and smiled. Sean/a's new neighbors had invited her for a holiday gathering. It was odd not having her around town, but this was the next step, and I was happy for her. She was making an effort to participate in the apartment BBQs and potlucks, always offering to bring a dessert or something special.

It wasn't always smooth sailing. She sometimes faced indignation from others at pool parties—from residents who took issue with Sean/a in her brightly colored bikinis and wigs. But thankfully, for the most part, people loved her willingness to join, to see and be seen, and to participate in the lively spirit of a communal gathering.

Sean/a fell in love with the "old Hollywood" glamour and the simultaneous calm of Palm Springs; it felt like home as it reminded her of living in Las Vegas during her senior year of high school and beyond.

Sean/a was dependent upon her own feet or the local bus system, which had a stop right outside the apartment. She rode the city shuttle every day and soon discovered various new "favorite spots" in town—hanging out at the local Starbucks, visiting a thrift store on Fridays, and even going to pro tennis events from time to time.

Because she is such a tennis aficionado, a friendly neighbor gave her tickets to the Indian Wells Masters tennis tournament. DeWayne helped her navigate that trip, and Sean/a, the ultimate tennis fan, thoroughly enjoyed herself. "A thrill of my lifetime," she told me afterward.

Once she moved to Palm Springs, we decided that regular housecleaning was no longer necessary. My housecleaner had been helping at her place every few weeks in La Jolla, but Sean/a had grown proficient at keeping her apartment tidy. Although her new living space was much larger than the studio apartment in La Jolla, we bought all the necessary supplies, and she was eager at the chance to keep her apartment immaculate.

She began to amass a bit of a wig collection, gathering gorgeous items from the thrift shop she visited every Friday like clockwork. "My friend Russell and the team there curate things just my size and fashion," she told me. "Imagine, dresses for two dollars, they are so kind to me." We had to have a discussion when she was spending more on new dresses than on groceries!

She also, it would seem, had broken her habit of giving everything away. She noted, "I used to get rid of everything. I never kept anything, always the clean slate, and then one day it hit me that the brain closet and the clothes closet are one and the same. Sometimes you need to keep a little for yourself." Without cluttering, she soon started sending me photos of a very cozy and homey apartment, with a closet full of outfits, shoes, and wigs. She had the courage to actually settle in somewhere.

I was grateful when she'd tell me how neighbors came through when she needed a few things or when her weekly money was spent a little early. She would always add something like, "There are so many people that have helped me in my life." Sean/a has a refreshing knack for remembering those who have helped her.

Although she had been housed for years, she recalled the challenging times, but always with a sense of gratitude. "I so appreciate the beautiful towels you gave me when we were decorating my new apartment. It reminded me of the other ones, half pink and half blue for Sean and Seana, that you ordered for me in La Jolla. A clean towel is everything to me! People have no idea what it feels like to shower and dry off with a fresh towel after living outdoors."

"It's different in Palm Springs," she observed. "I am not, nor have I ever been homeless here, and I don't go out, with the exception of parades, festivals, and during Pride events. I do my daily mood-walk therapy and Starbucks."

Several months after her move, she told me, "I am so thankful to live in a city in the beautiful desert where they prioritize caring about the LGBTQI community. It is safe, fairly nonjudgmental, and I don't stand out in a crowd … well, as much," she joked.

"I have made a lot of acquaintances," she added, "but I haven't been here long enough to create the lasting friendships I had in La Jolla."

"It'll take time," I messaged back.

Her messages reminded me that no home was going to be perfect, but each place had its own charm, its own style, and Palm Springs was proving to be a city that matched Sean/a's aesthetic and approach to life.

"In this inclusive LGBTQIA+ community, I feel like there is an understanding of what it means to have had one's body change. The mayor is forward-thinking about the challenges trans and intersex people face and she has been working hard to offer resources to people like me."

Mayor Lisa Middleton became a guiding light for Sean/a and spoke with her on numerous occasions regarding the rights of trans women, as well as trans and intersex safety. She also passed an innovative initiative that supported businesses such as El Pollo Loco, which gave hiring incentives to trans people.

This kind of freedom meant so much to Sean/a. She remarked, "It's hard to put into words what that means and how the fear of harassment, discrimination, violence, PTSD, and internal struggle can wreak havoc with the tasks of daily living."

When Sean/a's birthday rolled around, a trans musician friend at the local Starbucks sang her happy birthday. Little things like that made a huge impact on her and she reflected, "I hope everyone can find their own community. You reap what you sow, and I feel like in the desert community of Palm Springs, I have been able to reap goodwill and appreciation for just being authentically me."

When there was an intruder in her apartment complex, Sean/a quickly turned a potentially challenging situation into a new meet and greet in a different part of town. It happened to be Pride week, so she spent several days at a local hotel interacting with many interesting folks from all walks of life. Once safety had been restored, she reminded me that even in precarious situations, there was always a new perspective just around the corner, literally in this case.

~ ~ ~

The neighborly, good people in La Jolla missed Sean/a when she moved to Palm Springs. Plenty of La Jollans regularly visit Palm Springs on vacation, and Sean/a was frequently stopped on the street by those she'd known from her coastal community. These kind folks would then return to La Jolla bearing good tidings from Sean/a to all her "fans" and well-wishers who missed seeing her around town. She assured them all she was alive and thriving!

It made her realize how indelible a mark she'd left by her sheer act of joyously going about her day with the intention of contributing to the collective good.

CHAPTER 14

Both La Jolla and Palm Springs are vibrant cultural hubs where the arts flourish, and both embrace individual expression. Palm Springs has the unique distinction of being one of the most LGBTQIA-progressive communities in the nation, which is the foremost reason Sean/a chose it as her destination for the support and safety it could provide. And with its many athletic attractions to boot, Palm Springs grabbed Sean/a's attention in earnest.

She also loved the creativity of Palm Springs, and the connectedness of the community to a bygone era—mentioning her excitement, and of course taking a selfie (although it was often the other person who would initiate that request) when the grown children or grandchildren of movie stars would frequent old haunts.

Whether in spending time at festivals or local markets, she appreciated the tranquility of the desert life to gather her thoughts and have more time to reflect on herself, who she was becoming, and a myriad of other things.

~ ~ ~

It wasn't long before she became an essential voice for the community in Palm Springs. She got to know members of the local police departments and would inform them when she encountered anyone on her walks who might need assistance, or those who might be menacing to herself or someone else.

The police often followed up on her leads since she had become such a credible witness to the silent "under-the-radar" goings-on about town. As always, her goal was to aid in the betterment of the collective.

She learned the most efficient way to communicate with the local PD was via apps, hotlines, and the occasional text sent to the officers she knows best. She developed absolute faith through many years of experience that, for the most part, the police are there to serve and protect. She made it a point to inform the local police when she would be out of town for a few days, sure that someone would notice her absence as a valuable member of the community.

The specialized homeless outreach and liaison units were particularly fond of the working relationship Sean/a created with them to help her fellow citizens. The daily half-marathons she continued to walk—yes, even in the extreme desert heat of Palm Springs—made her ever ready for those who might need assistance.

One by one, the people who were initially intimidated by her living large and loud became her friends, eventually inviting her to Thanksgiving dinners and birthday parties. She also became the management's best security patrol, routinely helping them keep things under control—issues that Sean/a would notice on her lengthy walks or in her frequent conversations with residents.

Considering she walks half a marathon each day, she gets around every nook and cranny of the community of Palm Springs, just as she once did in La Jolla. Our texts back and forth remind me also of the importance of an active lifestyle. We joked that one day she might get sponsored by New Balance, Hoka, or Nike since we've certainly bought out their size 15/16 women's selection.

"I keep surpassing my fitness goals, Doc." Then came several screenshots of trophies. "Look at all these awards I get on my phone. My phone really knows me and challenges me."

"I wish I had a Sean/a app," I shot back. "You'd keep me on track, super fit, and it would reward me in positivity. It would say 'Praise' every time I reached my goals." I laughed to myself before adding, "Come to think of it, that's what your texts do."

"Maybe we can do that next, Kirst. I'd love to motivate people. Can you imagine?"

Yes, I can, actually! Sean/a's vision of establishing a walking sports ministry down the road is an aspirational call to pass on the benefits of fitness—not just physically, but emotionally and inwardly.

She continued formulating the idea for a motivational app: "Each day I would inform my readers how I live for well-being. I would share my daily journal of life and give them seven things to live by seven days a week. The key to learning is repetition, and as a community we could all get so healthy and fit. We could do this!"

I received texts from her in the heat of the summer, walking her way to nirvana but sweating in the crazy heat of Palm Springs, all the while offering a running commentary on the comings and goings of the community and its events. She regularly sent photos of the most random scenes—only accessible by walking hours daily on foot.

"How are your feet holding up?" I asked her recently.

"I have an old pair of sneakers," she said, "but I regularly change out the insoles from Walgreens, thank goodness."

I still have visions of her in the early days of our friendship—wearing feminine, size 10 flip-flops on her size 15/16 feet. Luckily, since then I've found perfectly fitting tennis shoes for her in a comfortable women's size 15/16, replaced when the pavement gets so hot the soles start to melt.

She has no problem noticing the extreme desert heat, although she still chooses to walk 12–15 miles a day even on days the temperature reaches 115 degrees. Sometimes, she opts to walk at night. When walking the deserted late-night streets, she can just think and breathe.

"People are curious why I stay in the desert when I'm such an avid walker and the summer is so scorching, but I truly love the tranquility and serenity and the open-minded culture," she messaged me. "Who knows where the wind will take me next."

Sean/a told me she was being referred to by some as the Walker of Palm Springs. She said, "That's all I do, every single day." She loved the peace she found in the desert where she was able to release all her troubles into the night air.

Another time, she texted me out of the blue, "Everyone in Palm Springs is so helpful. Even on the bus they all know me by name. It's so very special here; they truly care and have my back."

Overall, Sean/a's move to the desert was restorative and healing. She appreciated having a place where she could live more reflectively as well as more fully embrace who she is.

In La Jolla, after growing exhausted by being Sean all the time, Seana stepped up to embrace the new challenges of living as a female and picked up where Sean left off. In Palm Springs, she developed a true sharing of daily duties between Sean and Sean/a. When it got too warm for Seana's wigs, Sean's baseball hats took over.

In Palm Springs, she could be Sean or Seana without having to feel the expectations of being one or the other; her name represents both genders. She felt the freedom to wear bright pink sports bras and leggings with a bald head and a baseball cap. In the LGBTQIA+ community, she feels more at ease expressing herself as she wishes.

She once again existed in a category all unto herself, yet refused to let this get her down for long. Fortunately, there have always been enough good-hearted and like-minded souls around Sean/a who have seen her inner spirit and radiance to be in communion with her, liberating her from any lasting sense of isolation.

Notably, in San Francisco, DC, NYC, and LA, the first comments I always hear her make are about fitting in with the racial landscape and how refreshing it feels to be culturally attuned. Just as it is for many of us, the search for where she felt the most "spirit of place" was a lifelong quest. Pinpointing a particular "it" factor for the ideal community was an impossible task.

What struck me as most revealing was that every time we explored moving options, it was the relationships and routines she'd cultivated that she said she'd miss. In the end, the decision of whether to keep renewing her lease in Palm Springs came down to people. Of course.

While in one of her more reflective moods, she remarked, "One day far in the future, having a home here in Palm Springs sure would be nice. I may be old-fashioned, but the idea of sitting on my own little porch saying hi to friends sounds like bliss. Here I feel anything is possible."

For Sean/a, anything is possible.

She explained further, "I have some nice neighbors who invite me to BBQs, but for the most part people live in these apartments for a year or so and then they move on or buy a home."

I resonated with that desire for old friends and a strong community. After having lived in so many places, she deserved to have a lasting place to call home where she felt comfortable in her own skin and free to show up however she wished. I told her as much.

Sean/a responded with an even more contemplative observation. "Even though the changes going on in my body threw me off-track, I was actually on the perfect track for me."

Sean/a's move to a new city reminded me that the community is the thread that weaves together the individual, giving people permission to embrace their uniqueness and still feel welcomed.

Unfortunately, when Covid-19 hit, the world came to a standstill and suddenly everyone was stuck indoors. Sean/a was forced to find other ways to build community while confined in her one-bedroom apartment in Palm Springs.

Sean/a with Mayor Middleton

CHAPTER 15

Isolated

"The arts and humanities, the psychology of play, learning to imagine, it's all so important for the brain. Boredom creates anger. The pandemic made all of us isolated for two years, which felt especially hard in the desert."

~ Sean/a

Sean/a and I were recently talking about the importance of community. She commented, "Throughout the years I built a strong foundation of trust with my friendly neighbors. It came naturally to me. Then one day, I realized just how much we all needed one another."

"What made you come to that realization?" I asked.

She didn't hesitate to answer, "Covid."

Covid was a challenge for all of us, but I was especially concerned about how Sean/a would do under the restrictions. She was accustomed to riding the Palm Springs city shuttle on a daily basis—

heading to Starbucks or stopping by the local thrift store—but the shelter-in-place mandates halted the transportation for an indeterminate amount of time.

Covid also put a halt to the travel momentum she had garnered. Sean/a had been thrilled about the trips she'd been able to take. She'd loved discovering San Francisco, Sacramento, Santa Barbara, and NYC. We were planning the next trip when the restrictions hit.

Thankfully, true friendship revealed itself through Covid. Her friends made efforts to offer various activities that would keep her busy inside her apartment. Sean/a quickly found online church services to attend, which helped to reinforce her belief that she wasn't alone in this new challenge.

Phone calls were also a lifeline. Sean/a and I had long chats by phone, and we were both appreciative of the downtime to start our work on writing this book together—sharing many ideas and drafts back and forth.

When asked, she also allowed herself to be interviewed by phone to give people an understanding of her intersex condition and the challenges she had faced living on the margins of society. Folks asked her what messages she'd like to offer regarding her resilience and strength in adversity, which she was more than happy to share, and they then communicated to their church or greater community.

~ ~ ~

During Covid, Sean/a grew increasingly involved in online social media groups and chat rooms highlighting LGBTQIA issues and anti-bullying. With little else to do, her advocacy presence amped up. During the most isolative period of Covid—when people's stress, depression, and anxiety were at their peak—Sean/a grew alarmed at the amount of hatred and violence directed against various minorities, particularly trans women of color.

CHAPTER 15

It was if the virus had unleashed a pandemic of discrimination that had previously been swept under the proverbial rug. The divisive political climate only added fuel to the fire. People of color, trans people, and many Asians were targets of vicious hate crimes. These people weren't harassing anyone; there were no laws broken. Just being who they were elicited ire from those who had nowhere else to vent their frustrations and ennui.

Truly confused by society's seeming inability to live and let live, Sean/a befriended people online in an effort to immerse herself more deeply in their experiences and understand how their fears and concerns mirrored her own. She joined forces in various internet communities and rallied people around the cause of safety and protection for all.

As stories gained momentum in the media that showcased how the nation's cauldron of intolerance had reached a boiling point, Sean/a doubled down on her efforts to use social media platforms to draw attention and awareness to the plight of others just wishing to be themselves. She encouraged my teenage daughter and her friends to use their education and cultural awareness to effect broader change and focused on the importance of giving voice and power to the voiceless and the disenfranchised.

It was also interesting how Covid highlighted certain aspects of her life as a homeless person. For example, with people like Sean/a who didn't pay taxes yet really needed the stimulus checks, how would the government find them?

As the world stopped and people's focus turned inward and onto their immediate environs, I was acutely aware that Sean/a was by herself. I was concerned that the pressures on her would take a toll, especially being told she couldn't go outside for the long walks that served as therapy to her. Yet I found her even more open and willing to show care and concern for others.

It astounded me how quickly she used technology to keep connecting and building new cherished circles of trusting and engaged communities. Sean/a used online forums to inspire local heroes—the doctors, nurses, and those on the front lines—to keep fighting the good fight. Once, discussing the lack of personal protective equipment, she told me she had made her own masks.

"Actually, while I was out and about, someone gave me a difficult time, telling me that the mask I'd made was too small."

I just shook my head at that, knowing all the thought and effort that had gone into Sean/a creating a homemade mask for herself. She'd made it in a colorful pattern to try and bring a smile to others' faces, as well as allow her to safely and non-controversially exit her apartment and rejoin the public while still following the health guidelines.

As my daughter and I were busy accruing masks and protective equipment for my friends working the front lines via all sorts of international channels, Sean/a served as my eyes and ears in Palm Springs as well as many online venues, asking around to find those who might need them. As with many other circumstances in our ongoing friendship, we developed a great system wherein we followed up on each other's requests and brainstormed solutions collectively.

Sean/a was eager to get the vaccines when they became available. She was involved in planning her first vaccination when we hired private transportation to take her an hour's drive away, since that was the only place she could get in for an appointment. She then took her message of getting vaccinated and the benefits of being proactive directly online to the Black community, where she knew a trusted voice was needed. She did the same for the trans community.

CHAPTER 15

Once she understood how to register for her vaccine, she took matters into her own hands for the follow-up vaccines. She, in turn, helped an elderly person in her town navigate the vaccines. Covid highlighted the need for consistent support and concern for each other's well-being and health, and Sean/a surely rose to the challenge.

She told me, "Life sure was good before Covid," but then added, "we can give thanks for those vaccines."

After the most restrictive shelter-in-place mandates were lifted, and people were allowed to take walks—while masked, of course—Sean/a was back to her long desert walks. Always eager to find the positive in every situation, Sean/a reassured me over the phone that she would use the downtime of Covid to explore her new hometown of Palm Springs in an extended "staycation" of sorts.

I sent her boxes of Fiji water and Gatorade (thank God for Amazon) to take as she made her mood-walk rounds, and she began to take her surplus to feed the homeless in her role as "The Walker of Palm Springs."

It is remarkable how things had come full circle.

Slowly, as pandemic restrictions abated, we eased back into the travel routine we had been enjoying, first by scheduling a photo shoot in Newport and then Laguna Beach. Sean/a relished the chance to get a famous Balboa ice cream bar, which she'd last had forty years prior (on a trip to Southern California after high school graduation)!

A flood of happy memories was triggered by the sights, sounds, and tastes, which Kim captured beautifully with her lens.

Photo shoots in Palm Springs (my first time visiting her apartment) and back home to La Jolla were next. It was also the first time she and I had extended time together in the car to visit her old stomping grounds. I enjoyed the opportunity to invite her into my home.

I also had the good fortune of meeting those who had been taking such good care of her there in Palm Springs. She couldn't wait to pose at Revivals and introduce us to the staff. It felt very satisfying to be able to vouch for Sean/a that yes, indeed, we had been writing a book together and that her stories of being a co-author were valid.

She stayed a few days at the local Sheraton in La Jolla and, of course, left her mark. She then relayed an entire personal history with the hotel, from decades earlier, which really impressed upon me just how much life she had been living—productively, happily—until her rapid downward spiral.

After the photo shoots, I asked where she'd love to travel to for her upcoming birthday. She opted for Los Angeles, the city of her birth. I researched the famous W Hotel and decided the area with its trendy vibe and rife with tourist attractions would be perfect.

And it was. Not only did they provide her with a welcome bike to use—which she fearlessly navigated through traffic after many years without wheels—but they also wined and dined her, sending champagne and desserts to her room.

Seana had resumed her habit of walking long after nightfall and was heartened that there were many people still out and about in Los Angeles. She contemplated a move for the sake of this upcoming book's publicity, adding that she felt renewed with youthful vigor amongst all the "beautiful people" and "good-looking men" in the city.

She remarked that women were out past midnight pushing baby strollers and just communing with friends. It impressed her how there was such fluidity between the city and its residents. Again, she deeply resonated with the ethnic diversity and freedom to express her full self.

Seana felt completely comfortable in her own skin and was in her element in Los Angeles. She is, after all, a natural-born star.

I also took the liberty to buy Sean/a a plane ticket from Orange County to San Francisco to attend the musical "Tina!" based on the life of her idealized mom, Tina Turner. As with everything regarding Sean/a, I acted on impulse with this and never regretted the decision. Somehow, I knew this would heal some part of her soul to help her grieve Tina's transition from this earth.

Sean/a bought an elegant gown for the occasion and texted how emotional she was watching "Tina" on stage. She looked positively dignified and proper.

Old Hollywood glamour looked good on her.

~ ~ ~

Back at home, after a few-years-long absence due to Covid, Sean/a also accepted tickets I'd offered to watch the Alcaraz tennis match at Indian Wells, and she was entranced by the event.

"Doc, did you know many Americans aren't able to appreciate the small things because they are so busy? But oh my, at thirty dollars for a hot dog and fries, I'm amazed anyone can afford life. I must admit, they tasted as prestigious as the tennis."

She shared photos with me of the event. In the photos, she carried herself with dignity and poise. She was fully immersed and blended into the crowd, with rapt attention paid to the match. It touched me deeply to see how far she had come in her sense of belonging.

As the world emerged from its cocoon, I saw Sean/a's delicate wings emerge.

I recognized a change that had taken place in her. She no longer acted the outsider.

Perhaps she had found a place to call home.

CHAPTER 16

The Work of Rising Above

"So sad that with all the technology we have today and all the wonderful things we are doing, there's always still such tragedy that someone is victimized because of the color of their skin. African American trans women are at greatest risk."

~ Sean/a

I ran into Lili, an old colleague Sean/a had worked with at Vons years before. It explained why Sean/a had always felt so at home hanging out there. Of course, we got to talking about Sean/a.

Lili told me, "I have known Sean/a for decades and am impressed by her positivity and kindness, always with something nice to say about people. She was always a sun ray. Talking to her really brightened my day."

She went on to relate a memory of one day when she was working at Vons as a cashier. "Sean/a came in looking disturbed, and I knew something was going on. Then I saw this guy yelling at her with all sorts of profanities. Something took over me and I stepped out of the check stand and said, 'You stop that. Leave her alone.'"

"And what happened?" I asked, worried that Lili might have become the next subject of the man's ire.

"Everything in the store stopped suddenly. No one talked. Everyone was quiet. There I was, not even five feet tall, confronting someone acting very belligerent toward Sean/a. The guy left, and life continued." Lili shook her head. "Who knows what that guy would've done?"

"I'm glad you were there," I said. "What made you stand up for her like that, without hesitation?"

Lili smiled. "That was a no-brainer. Sean/a has created so much positivity around the community, so people are willing to stand up for her."

In Sean/a's life, there have been many people who tried to harm her dignity or misinterpret her actions, but thankfully, she has a gift for rising above.

Later, I asked Sean/a about her time working at Vons. She said, "The management and my coworkers understood me and how to best help when a situation created stress."

On one occasion, a customer was scared by one of Sean/a's louder moments. The woman ran and locked herself in the store's bathroom. She then pressed charges against Sean/a, but another customer testified in court on Sean/a's behalf. Thanks to her testimony, Sean/a was found not guilty.

"I realized how my behavior could be confusing or frightening to some, at times," Sean/a admitted. Sean/a understood that she had ultimate responsibility for her actions. Over time, she has learned to challenge herself to stay calm and not arouse panic in others, even when she has had to bear insults and harassment.

"It's important to have compassion on both ends," she remarked. "I try and honor the 'Teen Commandments' I had on my bedroom wall at college: to stand for something, treasure your time, and see what you can do for others."

Discrimination comes in many forms, and Sean/a often feels persecuted from the inside out as racial and mental health issues surface. The Black Lives Matter movement brought some overall cultural awareness, but Sean/a has consistently faced harassment.

Whether she's on a street curb or bus, Sean/a knows to steadfastly look straight ahead. She explained this as "an African American code switch not to deliberately alarm a white person in a wealthy community."

"It's all because of fear," she added. "That's what some of us go through every day. We're afraid, too." Existing intersex on the streets and facing daily harassment and discrimination, along with inner mental distress, Sean/a learned the importance of practicing dignity and optimism.

Sean/a has always lived in the margins—in gender, class, and mental health. As a six-foot, five-inch African American intersex collegiate athlete and coach with a huge personality, she has always been unable to hide. When she acted boldly, however, she was often told she was acting "out of bounds."

"Being African American ... boy, racism is something we deal with every day, and it's scary," Sean/a confessed. "We want to trust, but unfortunately, if there were a thousand good white people, there's going to be one bad one. That one bad one is going to make us afraid again. It's going to make us go and run back to where the fear came from."

~ ~ ~

I asked my ex-husband James, a Trinidadian American, his thoughts on relating to Sean/a's lived experience. James has long dreadlocks and is also a clean-cut, sharply dressed tennis pro and home developer. He could relate to Sean/a especially when it came to people's judgments.

He told me that many times (in our upscale, mostly white community) people would say things like, "There goes the Rasta guy. Let me ask him where to find the best weed in town."

James hasn't ever smoked a day in his life, yet here the stereotypical first impression follows him and branches out from there. He recalled growing up in jovial Trinidad, where people in the community who might have been perceived as "different" or outliers were still known as individuals and accepted accordingly. They were trusted, understood, and not automatically considered threatening. There was a shared compassion from being humanized.

He reminisced on beloved members of the community like "Mellow Mon" and "Cookie" and all the colorful characters who we would now refer to as flamboyant and gay, but back then they were just who they were, and everyone came over for a shared meal of laughter and good fun.

Upon moving to America as a teen, James recalled being advised that as a Black man, he was to show no weakness and not to show any behavior out of the norm. Anything that gave a person cause for pause or made someone wonder, "What's going on here?" was an automatic "That ain't gonna work in the Black community." Stretching boundaries of what people were slowly beginning to accept was a difficult stigma for many to move past.

James described how, once people's first impression of him set in, they often searched for something to reinforce their original bias. For example, "What kind of Rasta man are you if you don't smoke?" Additionally, having a white wife with his white stepdaughter and mixed-race children (my stepchildren) alienated him from both worlds.

After Trump was elected, the undercurrents of prejudice—even in our own neighborhood—were disappointingly unleashed. It is no wonder that James initially tried to distance himself from my involvement with Sean/a. He had already had enough controversy for a lifetime. Where I had felt a lack of support, he had viewed it as a threat to his and our family's well-being.

However, just as the community slowly changed one micro-interaction with Sean/a at a time, James began to feel solidarity with her struggle. He even took it upon himself to keep me posted when he had seen something untoward happening to Sean/a in order that I might be able to address it and help her.

James was taught—being a Black man in America, as opposed to Trinidad—that strength was measured by fitting in, not doing anything out of the norm. When he was teaching tennis to groups of affluent, predominantly Caucasian kids, playing reggae music on the courts, donning vibrant nontraditional tennis whites, was only acceptable because the "Rasta Tennis Academy" he founded was "cool." There was a shared understanding of trust and hip cross-cultural exchange appealing to teens. Of course, it helped that those kids were winning all the tournaments.

Throughout his career, his differences meant he had to work three times as hard to prove himself. James had the unfortunate experience early in his pro career as the lone Black player, of getting booed off the courts in Mexico. Only when he scored the first win for Trinidad and Tobago in the Davis Cup and began coaching at the Grand Slams did he finally feel legitimized in an arena in which winning transcended race.

Both James and Sean/a had, by necessity, learned to hone the skill of putting people at ease with humor. It gave people in tight-knit communities a chance to know who they were as individuals, enabling an exchange of goodwill instead of feeding into stereotypes and mistrust. Each learned to use standing out from the crowd as an advantage, yet it has taken both of them much inner strength and fortitude to stretch the boundaries of what society was willing to accommodate.

People like Sean/a and James have worked hard in finding ways to bridge the gap toward acceptance. As consistency bred comfort in its familiarity, perspectives such as "She's acting the fool" turned into "I see and respect you." When enough positive intention and behavior was captured in conversation, what started as an attitude of "You shouldn't be in our neighborhood" morphed into "We are lucky to have such genuinely good people in this town."

The bridge has been safely crossed, but there are more bridges ahead.

～～～

Sean/a is both a lightning bolt and a target. She grew up with a profound stutter and overcame her speech challenge through long years of speech therapy, but when she is stressed or openly discriminated against, it triggers her stuttering to this day.

This resultantly triggers her shame and humiliation from childhood. The struggle to verbalize is sometimes the only visible sign that she is overwhelmed. A microsecond later, thanks to a kind word from a stranger, she can be happily back in her zone of fluency.

As a stutterer, Sean/a suppressed some things she wanted to say as a child, some things she believed she should have said. This dichotomy caused her to avoid her inner self at times, resulting in confusion regarding who she truly was. Clearly, there was much more at play as well—issues that we've discussed in earlier chapters.

Seeing blatant discrimination against others was also a trigger, such as when she learned of the death of George Floyd. Flagrant, unreasonable violence simply made no sense to her, or to any of us, for that matter.

CHAPTER 16

When Aaron and I traveled to Minneapolis (my beautiful hometown) to see the George Floyd Memorial, Sean/a commented on photo after photo and sent many prayers. Considering her close connections with the police—a somewhat unusual stance for someone with her ethnic background—she was at once completely resonant with the Black community yet also understood the tensions that had long existed beneath the surface on both sides.

Sean/a's pacifist activism informs everything she does. Knowing of her quest for freedom for all from bondage and persecution, I sent her photos of local artwork, murals, and tourist banners as I traveled to places like Iceland, Europe, Germany, Chile, and Argentina. These works, depicting intolerance for bigotry and violence based on ethnicity, validated her own efforts in the United States. She was heartened that these messages were being espoused from far-flung and sometimes unexpected locations around the globe.

~ ~ ~

Sean/a makes a difference just by showing up as her authentic self. She honestly approaches each friendly interaction with a benevolent and peaceful, inquisitive heart. She has always known her story would carry a message much greater than herself. The success she envisions for this book is not about her. It is on behalf of all those individuals whose struggles have thus far gone unnoticed, whose tales are begging to be acknowledged.

She has made a concerted effort to put the help and support she's received to good use in advocating for others. She advocates practicing patience regarding changing the mindset of the masses one social media post at a time. (Although Sean/a credits "effort" as the number one reason she currently has great physical health and mental stamina, she is acutely aware of the role other people have played in her overall safety and well-being.)

Sean/a has overcome countless obstacles and implicit biases, and continues to move forward as an incredible example of hope and perseverance. Just by her sheer humanity, she lifts people up. She is a quiet (and at times loud) activist just by showing up authentically as Sean/a every single day.

Her message of inclusion and anti-bullying has primarily centered around intersex and male-to-female trans rights as well as the safe, peaceful existence she has worked so hard for, free of harassment.

Sean/a is genuinely intrigued by my daughter's generation, calling them the most influential in determining the shift in perception and stigma regarding LGBTQIA+ individuals and their right to life, liberty, and the pursuit of happiness. The current zeitgeist has embraced a spirit of understanding and openness, and I am grateful for it.

As a side note, Sean/a never looked so peaceful and serene as during the annual gay pride week celebrations in Palm Springs, when the already very tolerant and accepting LGBTQIA+ community becomes even more hospitable and welcoming. She has regularly expressed gratitude for the ability to live in such a safe, tolerant, and accepting community.

Sean/a and I both advocate for effecting change via a "compassionate underground" of sorts wherein one's support team rallies around when everything is at stake. An individual's challenging life transitions are facilitated with the help of one person at a time until it's the next person's turn to help. Isn't this what is at the heart of a community?

She has also parlayed her police involvement into her new life in the desert, where concerned citizens can earn points on an app, tracking who is engaging with the Riverside County Sheriff's office. Gone are the days when people could just turn a blind eye, and—as in many other areas—Sean/a is leading the way with community support in this respect as well. (Last I heard she was ranked fourth in the community app for citizen watch!)

CHAPTER 16

In online chat groups as well, Sean/a harnesses coping skills born of her own trying circumstances in helping others to heal or advocate for themselves. Her civic duties, citizenry, and social services keep her very active—whether it be in cyberspace, on the bus, on her walks, or in community hangouts she frequents. She offers solutions to those who, like her, have often faced discriminatory practices or endangerment.

Sean/a was once kicked out of a transitional housing space for transgender individuals. She hadn't been aware it was a sober living facility and had brought in Nyquil for a cold, which promptly resulted in losing her place of safety and refuge. She has since taken action by writing posts on the websites of relevant organizations to effect change regarding arbitrary guidelines, costing someone their only safe haven. She tries incessantly to make life relatable.

Sean/a didn't seek out any sort of celebrity status. In one respect, she has spent her adult life being sought out, harassed, ridiculed, and misunderstood. Yet she has turned that around to control her own narrative, hoping to shed light on fundamental truths regarding identity and belonging, acceptance and self-esteem.

Sean/a embodies the Law of Attraction. She vibrates at such a high frequency and her positivity draws people in.

"To thine own self be true," as the famous quote from Hamlet goes, or as Ziggy Marley's ringtone on my phone happily announces Sean/a's texts, "You've got to be true to yourself." Sean/a has spent a lifetime trying to understand who that self is. She fits in both everywhere and nowhere. She can be alone but not lonely.

She has described herself as needing people. Once, several of us were chatting together and a friend of hers said to Sean/a, "You really are fascinating. Even the church doesn't have an answer for you. What can they say?"

I cut in with this answer: "That you are a great human being and more ethical than most."

"I love neighborly, good people," Sean/a added. "If we could all stop and smell the roses, or at least try and help others by being grateful, kind, and compassionate ... wow."

Years into our friendship, Sean/a still takes a photo of her stocked fridge weekly and sends it to me along with a "thank you" text. Whenever the local thrift shop puts something aside for her or reduces the price to next to nothing, she gleefully exclaims in a text to me, "One man's trash is Sean/a's treasure ... and boy, do I treasure. How kind of them to think of me."

She meaningfully sets the intention to remain deeply in touch with her core, yet never takes the path of least resistance. Sean/a holds the community accountable by her nonviolent act of stoically absorbing what is swirling around her while trying not to get caught up in it.

No matter the positivity she exudes, though, there is still the social reality that she is always trying "to assimilate to a world which fears black bodies," as Alua Arthur eloquently states in her heartfelt memoir, *Briefly Perfectly Human*. Arthur continues, "In tense moments, I know I stand a better chance of surviving conflict if I make myself small and unthreatening, and if I quiet myself down so that I am not deemed rowdy or scary."[15]

Add to this the reality of intragroup discrimination and it's no wonder Sean/a has decided to transcend the completely double-bounded reality of her existence and rewrite the script on her terms. Her spiritual principles, compassion, community spirit, neighborliness, and friendliness lead the way.

---

15 Alua Arthur, *Briefly Perfectly Human* (Mariner Books, 2024), 95.

Sean/a made up a term to describe when people get uncomfortable around her; she calls it Intersex Panic Disorder. She said it activates "when people think they can handle the reality of me and being with me ... but then they back out."

She added, "Transphobia is real." Even in this realm about which she feels so strongly, she manifests this perspective of understanding: "Look, we all have fears. I remember the teachings at the Boys and Girls Club, how to laugh at things you don't understand instead of lashing or acting out."

Sometimes she acts outrageously according to onlookers, but they haven't been privy to the numerous injustices that have occurred to finally push her off her center. As she nurtures herself and renews her sense of tranquility, her serenity returns as she finds herself coping with more flexible strategies. Her higher mind (or perhaps her Inner Self Helper) guides her toward whatever creative solution is warranted, and she trusts this guidance implicitly.

It goes without saying that Sean/a is impossible to miss. Therefore, when she's standing tall and carrying a large "stop intersex surgery" sign, it gets one's attention. Just as effective, however (perhaps even more so), are the moments when I watch her in action animatedly engaging curious tourists. I watch their heads bob up and down in an affirmation of whatever Sean/a is surely teaching them on the importance of nondiscriminatory practices, especially against intersex and trans populations.

I literally see her growing more centered during such interactions, completely certain that this is her life's mission, her platform. And still she rises.

Interestingly, when Sean/a had presented in La Jolla as Sean, people perceived him as strong and competent and were not nearly as helpful or accommodating as when Seana came out. Seana elicited more concern and sympathy, less fear, and was considered approachable and nonthreatening. She definitely garnered the support of the community—especially females—more than Sean, as kind and nonthreatening as he was.

As Sean, there was an assumption of competence.

As Sean/a, warmth and friendliness.

Interestingly, an older African American male checker at Von's always referred to Sean as "the brother" for years even when she was dressed as Seana. I wondered if this was due to the "cultural bias" that James referred to still in place.

As James stated previously, disarming people involved holding the tension of two opposing truths. One was the personal conviction and strong sense of self both he and Sean/a share; the other, a deep awareness at all times that they know their role in society. Balancing such tensions in tandem isn't easy. Both individuals garnered deep respect as athletes, a trait that holds value in our fitness-based culture. James disarms with his friendly Caribbean demeanor, while people are charmed by Sean/a's optimistic outlook and positive attitude.

When people are marginalized, especially on an ongoing basis, they have the opportunity to transcend all groups. But it's not easy. The notion of betraying one's race comes into stark play when one's individualism contradicts racial edicts. Often, the community at large refuses to appreciate individual expression.

In her memoir, Arthur refers to the "oppressive erasure which does not acknowledge, among other things, that Black people's strength is evidenced by the ability to surrender without being broken."[16] There's a meta-understanding that happens when someone has been misunderstood for so long. Rising above becomes a survival tactic.

---

16 Arthur, *Briefly Perfectly Human.*

CHAPTER 16

In Sean/a's case, rising way far above. Once a person realizes they can never "win" in the current game that is being played, leaving the playing field altogether and creating their own "game" appears the sensible, sane, survival-based option. And sure enough, building one's own field of dreams invites others to come to play in this newly imagined space.

The ultimate goal is no more cliques, no more alienation, no more artificial divisions. The grandiosity that keeps people separate, when turned to humility, allows all to belong. The heartfelt warmth that emanates from vulnerably standing in one's own truth enhances the well-being of self and the entire community, bringing individuals and subcultures together.

I see Sean/a standing in her truth, and her words inspire me.

"I never carried around Sean and Seana; I was always one or the other. Today I feel I am Seana, and I feel light. I'm not trying to be a woman; I am a woman. As much as I lived fifty years as a man. The joy comes from inside and knowing I have civil rights which allow me to express myself as I am."

The LGBTQIA+ community has always been supportive of Sean/a. They have respected her courage to be her unfiltered self in seemingly uptight, upscale communities. As an intersex individual, she feels her true female part of self might threaten some individuals. She has experienced this dynamic in groups, and it truly pains her, as she wants everyone to know they are as fully male or female as they see themselves and wish to be. She feels perplexed by this behavior and wishes everyone could just peaceably coexist.

As Sean/a puts it, "Black lives matter, trans lives matter, and intersex lives matter."

Sadly, even in the educated, liberal communities where she's lived, there are still the occasional bad apples, particularly teenaged males, who have harassed her mercilessly, goading her and calling her racially-motivated and gender-targeted slurs. Throughout it all, Sean/a continues to treat the community as her extended family.

James has also had his share of obstacles and misperceptions to contend with on a daily basis, but both he and Sean/a face these misattributions as opportunities to inform the public.

As stepmom to a mixed-race, special needs child who can only be described as one of the world's most endearingly charismatic and charming humans, I have often been approached by kind strangers whose eyes convey an attitude of "Bless you, white woman, for adopting this clearly challenged but wonderful child," to, "Oh, she's your stepdaughter? You are a mixed-race family?" followed by glances laden with judgment.

When my biological and white daughter, a high-level athlete, would do her morning workouts with her stepdad, James, they would get "concerned" looks from others when she would call him "Dad" or give him a post-workout hug of appreciation. James could've easily grown bitter and reinforced the stereotype, but instead he would greet those same people with the all-good, big-ups hand sign—a common good morning gesture in Trinidad.

Slowly, but surely, people's expressions would change. They might even return the greeting with a smile or ask questions about their workouts and how they might get some high-level training as well.

I share Sean/a's prayers and deep faith that, through her courage and vulnerability, other lives can be deeply changed. We envision a world with all people standing in solidarity on behalf of everyone's right to dignity and free expression, to live their truths, and to be protected and deeply heard.

My wish is that all people may use the power of their voice through their stories and the way they boldly live their lives to empower others to stand tall and be free from violence, oppression, hatred, and judgment. My deepest hope is that people will take these examples of positivity, faith, and hope, and strive to live the best life possible during our limited time on earth, building community wherever they go.

~ ~ ~

Sean/a has a special title for herself and other people she's met for whom she has deep respect: MEPs, Maximum Effort People. Clearly, she stands out as one! She brought a smile to my heart when she included my hard-working daughter, Tia, in that category when she rallied to help organize vaccine appointments and transportation for Sean/a during Covid.

Another MEP, Sarah—her wonderful resume builder and helper—facilitated Sean/a's channeling of community extracurriculars into viable work history. Projects such as these from the mutual goodness of people's and Sean/a's hearts, have helped her maintain strong relationships with local entities.

Bishop's School is one such example, where ladies she knew on campus supported her quest to follow up on coaching in the community and the inquisitive, courageous students interviewed her for their local newsletter, bringing legitimacy and visibility to Sean/a's plight. Their humanitarian approach was validating and heartening as the next generation advocated for Sean/a and others who struggled.

She told me, "You can't build a church alone," reiterating that she's never alone. "Once, I was walking down the street when a car pulled up next to me on the sidewalk. It was Brent from the La Jolla Tennis Club asking me how I was coping with the cold weather."

"And how were you coping?" I asked.

"Well, I had just taken my morning shower at the beach, with cold water and no towel."

I cringed at the thought. "That doesn't sound like fun."

"He generously handed me his white snowboard jacket that he had just used on the ski slopes of California."

Sean/a looked at me, earnest in her expression. "That's what I mean about never being alone. That gesture has always stood out in my mind as so very kind. It meant so much to me. People are so busy and sometimes we forget to ask how someone is doing. It made my day. After that, Brent had tennis shoes, shorts, and T-shirts for me in the spring weather, and we've been friends ever since."

"And then there was Doug." I reminded her of another example of reciprocity.

"Doug," she repeated, smiling. Her friend Doug was a jazz lover who enjoyed visiting New Orleans. "He was one of the nicest people you ever met," Sean/a continued. "He was very quiet and minded his own business. He was a gentleman and loved to go swing dancing. He talked about his love for dancing."

When Doug had been seriously injured in a horrendous attack, Sean/a was all too willing to help. "You know, I used to collect spare bottles and cans Doug left for me, to earn extra change. So, when I was able to donate to Doug's GoFundMe, when I was able to wish him well, it meant so much to have the ability to do that."

She smiled and I felt lifted up by her generosity and deep concern for others. "People rally around people's character, you know?" she said. "That's why the support for him was there when he needed it. He had great character."

"It's amazing how the friends you have made stayed with you through the years," I observed.

"Reunions and reconnecting with others are truly a privilege," Sean/a replied. "You never know if you might need someone's help one day. Black, white, LGBTQIA or whatever, learn to love and forgive as much as you can."

As a community joiner and icon, Sean/a has been blessed to find that, often, those who initially misunderstood her slowly grew to become her staunchest allies, and vice versa. Sean/a cherishes those friends and advocates whom she considers acting from the deepest levels of courage, being willing to go out on a limb for her and others who reside in the margins.

She has been a personal trainer, aerobics instructor, basketball coach, dance instructor, and nanny—all from connections she made on and off the streets. And now she has had the privilege of showing up for these same friends in a neighborly, genuinely full-circle compassionate manner.

It's all about reciprocity, community, inclusion, and humility. When we extend goodwill, we never know when we might be blessed to be the receiver.

We all rise, together.

CHAPTER 17

Reflections

"We tell the stories that need to be told. I always knew there was somebody with me, a higher guiding force, because every time something happened, I was pulled out every step of the way. ... We are called in life to pay it forward."

~ Sean/a

Sean/a has a gift that is "hallmark Sean/a." She can weave together the most disjointed ideas and make them sensible, stringing together disparate concepts from discrete states of consciousness. This makes our collaboration as authors an interesting one, to say the least.

Pretty much every time we met for a smoothie to gather information about her life's history or details about her journey, we found ourselves off topic. Yet this new tangent was usually far more interesting than the original subject. Spurred on by a comment from a passerby about her outfit, or the many people from all strata of life who would stop and tell her hello, there was never a dull moment and never a conversational lull.

The integration of ideas and her meta-concerns were juxtaposed with the mundane. For instance, when I let go of the reins while asking about a phenomenon of consciousness, Sean/a might launch into a spontaneous conversation about wigs and which ones were most comfortable, or how the cut and style mattered. She would inevitably tie this into the conversation at large and come up with a profound truth about identity and what it was like to be able to shift one's perception and alter one's state of consciousness depending upon the choice of hairstyle.

Watching Sean/a swish her hair with the back of her hand and posture with a huge "I'm on camera" smile as she stayed completely connected to the conversation reminded me this was a woman with a true gift in the art of human relations. Through dialogue, the discovery unfolded like an admixture of different instruments in a symphony … coupled with a generous dash of improv comedy.

Our deep dive into her inner struggles, while often infusing a breath of fresh air into challenging topics, also brought things to the surface that could potentially destabilize her. I learned to be careful to let her initiate the topic of conversation. Sometimes I just sat back and listened as Sean/a shared true wisdom.

"What does belonging mean to you?" I asked Sean/a as we sat at our usual table, watching the world go by and Sean/a interfacing with it in her own unique way.

"Oh, plenty of things, Doc. I belong everywhere and nowhere at the same time."

I waited for her to clarify what she meant.

"We all want approval, right?" she added. I nodded to confirm. "We're all about wanting to belong to someone or something. But I think the biggest challenge for me is learning to keep loving myself. I need to belong to myself first. That has to come first."

"It does," I agreed.

"Belonging is a big part of me, and I love to be a friend. I would love to be a part of a family or a friendship, but I have to work on myself. I ask myself, 'What are my values, what is my sense of worth, how can I help other people?'"

"Those are important questions to ask," I said, amazed once more at how someone so gregarious was simultaneously so reflective.

Sean/a continued, "I'm someone who I think has earned the right to be in society; I loved being a part of teams and sports, schools, and coworkers. Community. That's the ultimate form of belonging, but it's not always easy."

"You have a knack for belonging in all sorts of places," I remarked.

She shrugged. "I enjoy being a friend. It's why I like to belong to groups on social media. I learn from them; they learn from me. When I was in fourth grade, I decided I wanted to be a PE teacher like Mr. Ashton. I just wanted to teach and inspire kids to reach their Presidential Fitness awards and enjoy field day."

"You knew what you wanted to do at that young age?" I was impressed. Sometimes it takes so long for a person to decide what they want to do in life.

Sean/a nodded. "But it wasn't just about the games. It's about teaching respect, like, 'You do your thing, I'll do mine, and even if I don't like everything you do, you've got it going on,' you know?" She glanced at me to make sure I was tracking. I nodded my understanding.

"I think that pretty much sums up my whole life," she said with a laugh. "Live and let live. And ask me if you are confused. Often, I am too, but we can figure it out together."

After a brief yet enthusiastic interaction with a passerby who stopped by our table, she turned her attention back to our conversation.

"If you know something is inside of you, inside of your heart or your mind that doesn't make sense yet, you've got to persevere. Be persistent. Don't give up if you know it's what you are living for, the purpose of why you're here on earth." She paused and took a sip of her green smoothie.

I had learned better than to jump in with my two cents when she was getting to the core of some topic, so I waited for her to continue.

"Whether it's to help your neighbor or help the country or whatever, don't give up. That's something I went through being on the street, literally not knowing what each day would bring, being blamed for things I didn't do, even facing the criminal justice system."

"You've been through a lot, Sean/a," I agreed. "It's remarkable how you haven't let that hurt your ability to connect with others."

"I love people," she answered. "My school, my church, my community, and abiding by the laws of that community."

With a big smile, Sean/a waved at someone across the room who was leaving the restaurant. Swirling the straw around her cup, she continued, "For a long time, it felt like no one bothered to really care about how I was doing or whether I was holding things together. It's important to acknowledge people who may be struggling and just say, 'Hi, how are you, how is life?'" She blinked a few times. "You did that, Kirst, and it made all the difference for me."

"It made a difference to me, too," I told her.

"We make a good team."

With this project, Sean/a embraced the chance to enhance kinship with her fellow humans, stand in her empowerment, and manifest a healthy sense of pride despite all she has suffered through and risen above. Other benefits of this book she hopes for include reducing stigma and offering her the chance to stand up for the disenfranchised, which appeals to her altruistic nature.

She appreciates the opportunity to convey how she has grown and healed from dark moments in her past. Regarding her childhood, she reflected, "I always had to know my place, to submit. It was always a part of me growing up while being African American. I felt loneliness with my intuition and my gender ambiguity. Social loneliness set in at times when I felt I just couldn't explain myself, either to myself or to others."

True to Sean/a, her moment of reflection gave way to a genuine smile and an exclamation of gratitude. "My, how times have changed."

"What changes stand out the most to you?" I asked eagerly.

She leaned forward, eyes bright, fully engaged. "When I lived in the village of La Jolla and walked everywhere, I started meeting all sorts of interesting, diverse people from all different backgrounds and countries, and they all seemed to belong. I started to feel as if I belonged as well."

"Maybe seeing that diversity around you helped you to embrace the diversity within," I suggested.

"And now in Palm Springs, I just think of how many people I've met over the years. I started the Walking Club because it gave me a chance to spend quality time with some of the people I've met in town who could also get to know one another. Nice people from around the globe."

I reflected on the mood-therapy walk I had taken with her and several other women, the day she left me with the word "joy" to carry through the week. "You do have a gift of connection, Sean/a."

"If we could all take the time to remember we are all connected, we are all community, what a difference that would make." She threw her arms out wide. "I love everyone; I guess I'm just high on life."

Sean/a has a gift of helping people open up via discussions, by sharing her own vulnerabilities and various adaptations to this highly stressful existence, unrelenting in its pressures and expectations. I believe anyone who allows themselves to has learned a thing or two from Sean/a's ability to take it all in stride (in her case, very large strides).

Her perspective weaves together the years of her past journey with the sage wisdom of her present, providing her with a remarkable vantage point. Sean/a's individuation during moments of deconstruction and re-enchantment with her daily life have also been instrumental in pushing her ever forward. She embraces her connections with nature, music, exercise, art, and the benevolence of those around her to make up for the years spent with a paucity of resources.

~ ~ ~

To this day, the flow of our interactions is a delicate balance nearly ten years in the making. We have a natural understanding and ability to connect and go as deep as Sean/a wishes or requires. The foundation of trust, reliability, and consistency has been forged one micro-interaction at a time. All I can say is that our personalities and life missions have been uniquely cleaved together and could only have been laid down by a divinely ordered plan.

Sean/a is unafraid to challenge me in my efforts to articulate the ineffable. She has redirected me when I have gone astray in my assumptions or attempted more tangential inferences. My presuppositions about her life were false at times, and when this was the case, my erroneous assumptions about her mental state or physical condition were noted and redirected in the service of healing.

As I backed away from a more confining role, paradoxically, the concept I was in search of spontaneously emerged as an effortless flow. Sean/a has been instrumental in raising consciousness regarding tolerance and allowing things to exist as they are without forcing premature awareness. This has been a true educational process for me.

As co-authors and co-researchers, we have surmounted many obstacles together on this journey. Each of us is evolving in our freedom of expression and how we relate to each other's exercise of it. I am learning the importance of simply bearing witness and honoring her struggle. This is what it means to simply and truly "be" with another person.

Acceptance appears as it needs to for each of us. If we look for it in a particular location or shape, it will necessarily elude us.

On our recent trip back and forth to Palm Springs and La Jolla for a book cover photo shoot, we conversed for hours at length about life and all its permutations. We toured all her old neighborhoods and sent her sister some photos while Sean/a shifted rapidly between the factual and the philosophical. I was privy to the inner workings of her mind and her elephantine memory for detail.

All the stories she had relayed over the years regarding doctor's appointments, where she first got an ID, the government physical exams regarding her intersex condition, her favorite hangouts and wig stores, came to life with great clarity and honesty. It was heartening to retrace her footsteps and it reminded me that each of us has a journey that is unique and full of twists and turns.

She was effusive with ideas about how to synthesize all that she had learned from her own experience and that of others at the Gay and Lesbian Center and her desire to offer it as a course on gender studies at the university. Sean/a has set this as a solid goal for herself, excited at the thought of creating a curriculum.

She said, "I would love to develop a course curriculum teaching kids about resilience, belonging, and how to survive and thrive through adversity and, of course, teaching tolerance and acceptance for gender, racial, and socioeconomic differences. Most importantly, having compassion for those who are labeled as different."

It was during college that she'd first been given a book and was talked to about the topic of homosexuality. Hers was a spiritual wrestling at the time, having been raised with strict Baptist rules and ideas. The renewal of her deep faith over the years has been a consistent well of strength she wishes to share with young people who are internally conflicted about their identities.

"In the end, we are all different, and that's what makes us beautiful."

I don't think anyone could say it better.

~ ~ ~

It is truly remarkable when I think back to our evolving relationship and how much life has transpired between us. She still sends me texts daily on every conceivable topic. In fact, I get most of my news and esoteric research articles from her. I am fascinated, amused, educated, enlightened, and everything in between by her insights and choice of videos, musings, or stories she shares.

I might have started out as the encouraging and supportive listener, friend, mentor, and teacher; yet she has returned all the aforementioned in equal manner.

Throughout our ongoing interactions, I was very aware of the importance of good boundaries (perhaps hyperaware, at times). As much as it pained me in the beginning, I obliged my ex-husband's request to not have Sean/a in our home or car—a rule I only recently "broke" after nine years. These rules necessitated my begrudgingly asking Sean/a to have to walk everywhere to meet me (before Uber was a thing) and paying massive taxi fees to the airport for travel and to relocate her when she moved to Palm Springs.

Sean/a has been privy to my shifting life story through family rearrangement, divorce, health crises, Covid, and my daughter connecting with her biological donor father, Aaron, through 23andMe (who moved in with us for a time—a story for another book)! This was the Aaron who, after hearing of Sean/a's wish to reconnect with her roots, took her on a tour of her old hometown in Colorado.

There has been no shortage of dramatic plot twists. In comparison, at times, her journey has appeared much more stable and "normal." Funny how life is.

I think about Sean/a's dissociative schizophrenia as well as how her intersex condition classifies her as having a rare medical disorder, and I consider what this unique combination of extreme challenges has been like for her. How frustrating it must be to fall outside the realm of understanding and helpful medical intervention time and again!

In a small way, I feel a measure of her frustration when I realize that only .007 out of one million individuals in the adult population have the disorder I was diagnosed with. This rarity makes medical help and treatment feel elusive, experimental, and generally as if I need to become the expert on my own condition.

Although oddly symptomatic, I have only been aware of my condition for five years. It is not socially visible and ofttimes when people hear of it, they are curious and sympathetic—unlike the common responses to Sean/a's condition. She usually faces curiosity and assumptions at best and misunderstanding and judgment at worst.

I was also, thanks to my mother's lineage, blessed with another rare condition called synesthesia, in which I process numbers and letters as colors. My mom's version even positions these colorful letters and numbers localized in space. As a young person, this "gift" procured advantages in learning languages due to their associations. I readily picked up French, German, and Spanish and couldn't understand when studying Russian with its completely different alphabet that I was in the same boat as the general population.

In this manner as well, I can relate to some aspects of Sean/a's condition as fascinating to some. I can't tell you the amount of times I've been quizzed up and down by people trying to get a grasp on my condition or trip me up. An astute professor of mine at Georgetown, Dr. Daniel Robinson, even posited a link to dyslexia because my 3s and Es were both yellow, my 2s and "S" were both green, and my 4 and its alphabetic inverse "h" were both lavender, etc. Nonetheless, classmates were as perplexed and enthralled as ever.

There is such a fine line between curiosity and being cast as an outsider.

I was starting to really understand how the sheer visibility of Sean/a's differences was a force she had to vigilantly manage.

We meander through these murky, uncharted rare medical waters together. As I've become more aware of the challenges that a lack of understanding and awareness have caused her, I marvel at the courage she has shown over many years—facing not only misunderstanding but also adversity, which precluded getting the appropriate care.

We both live in uncertainty and face misinterpretation. Sean/a has consistently channeled her emotions into advocacy, using her empathy to make a difference for others navigating similarly challenging deep waters.

People don't choose homelessness. They don't choose identity struggles or gender ambiguity. They don't choose chronic illness or mental disorders. There are stories of struggle and resilience, coping and surviving behind every statistic.

Our hope is that through getting to know Sean/a via this book, you will want to discover the stories of individuals behind the statistics, that you will be moved to a deeper level of understanding and compassion, and that this renewed empathy will bring about change in the world.

One story, one life, at a time.

CHAPTER 17

With survivorship—such as that which Sean/a has demonstrated—appears to come a sense of responsibility to temper the effects of cruelty by offering some sort of guarantee to future generations. A guarantee that acts of atrocity have not happened in vain and that every possible action will be taken to prevent them from happening again. Creating a just society based on mutual liberties and understanding requires a thoughtful, more utilitarian approach.

Sean/a is highly committed to anti-bullying and standing up for LGBTQIA+ rights. She uses her coaching and teaching knowledge to influence the younger generation on safety and self-expression. Her goals include helping disseminate knowledge around defending the transgender and intersex community's right to exist peaceably and for its youth to have a voice.

There is a basic fear at the root of society that is fostered by ignorance and avoidance, often practiced by those who should lead the public in a quest for awareness. Yet when an enlightened society allocates its resources to those who have suffered trauma or been relegated to the fringes, the collective strength of the individual joined with the group facilitates an advancement of knowledge and spiritual growth.

Recognition, witnessing, validation, and support—all these, in time, have the power to turn the tides of justice in favor of those who have so unjustly suffered.

〜 〜 〜

I have watched Sean/a develop into a much more settled, refined version of who she is since she no longer has the continual stress of finding her next meal or living with the burden and stigma of being unhoused. Following her move to Palm Springs, I have been inspired to see her continuing to blossom into a uniquely joyful and exuberant being with a true sense of belonging.

The mutual space Sean/a and I have created over the years has been filled with heightened interest and sensitivity for safe exploration. In this space, our relationship has been given a chance to unfurl naturally and beautifully. I am often surprised and in awe at what is continually revealed.

Sean/a is forthright in her presentation of the facts of her life and has provided the same details over and over lest I misunderstand. She was less interested in preconceived ideas about mental struggles and homelessness and more interested in the thought-provoking discussions around living life as intersex and how society needs to examine its biases and provide resources to those who couldn't even take their sex for granted.

Her dynamic life force—a spiritual energy not bound or contained—is in part the result of bravely questioning those in authority and delving into established teachings for a more holistic understanding that fits her life's trajectory. Sean/a's valiant efforts to better understand her place in family, community, society at large as a world citizen, and in the universe offers a glimpse of one woman's extraordinary journey.

Somehow, through her guidance, the vastness and complexity of life seems less intimidating and more comprehensible, meaningful, and purposeful. Her hope and joy in living simply inspires us to look for the sacred in everyday life and practice the art of transcending beyond any limitations imposed from without—and more importantly, from within. From her perspective, humans are evolving to become that which at its heart is most purely loving and compassionate.

When joy and optimism banish fear, when the cleansing of accumulated negative experiences takes place, we create a virtuous atmosphere wherein deep healing is facilitated. Once the hurting members of a community are empowered to thrive, when survivors have been fortified with purpose, all things become possible.

CHAPTER 17

One of Sean/a's most impactful biblical reminders is "If you lose your life for what is right, you will find it; if you save your life, you will lose it." Survivors may have missed essential learning tasks of daily existence, but in their stead, they have fostered and cultivated a transcendent awareness with far-reaching implications.

In Sean/a's case, it appears she has risen like the Phoenix.

With angel investor friend, Lisa

Sean/a's 50th birthday

CHAPTER 18

Deep Belonging

"We can't do this life all on our own. We need one another. My family and friends have been such a part of my journey of gaining the wisdom and wealth of knowledge to educate others. That's why I'm here; I'm here to serve."

~ Sean/a

"**D**oc, thank you for all the things you got me during your travels," Sean/a said when we met up after my return from a trip overseas.

I was confused by her comment, as I had only brought her a single scarf. "What do you mean?"

"It was how I knew I could trust you," she continued. "You would go places and then give me beautiful purses and clothes and scarves from around the world. I was in awe of all those designers." The unspoken content was, "You didn't forget about me while you were gone."

I realized she was referring not to my most recent trip but journeys I had taken in the past. I delighted in being able to bring Sean/a little trinkets from different parts of the world I hoped she could one day see with her own eyes.

"It was your smile and tone of voice, too. Your presence assured me that I had a future." She paused for a second. "We've been through so much together, Doc. Remember when your daughter baked and sent me intersex-themed Christmas cookies with pink and blue sugared sprinkles? That was the Christmas when Hilary's daughter, Haley, helped me set up my first Christmas tree. Bless the kids for thinking of me during the holidays."

"They're not kids anymore." I laughed. "Time has flown by."

Sean/a was still in full reminiscent mode. "And Cecile's daughter, Grace, was always so welcoming and polite, with her British accent and her gift of hospitality. When we did the fundraiser at their tea house restaurant, she made me feel so dignified."

"I remember." Was that really almost a decade ago?

"And Aaron making sure I had time to fully connect with my roots on the Colorado homecoming trip he graciously organized." She sighed deeply. "Good-hearted people affirm what I have always known."

"And what's that?" I asked.

"That we are here to care for one another on this journey of life."

It's been quite a journey together, that's for sure.

I don't know how to adequately convey the impact of our lives on each other. How could I have known that ten years ago, a momentary flash of heart-opening conviction to do whatever it took to help Sean/a find shelter would result in an inexplicable connection forged through adversity and triumph, but most importantly through friendship?

CHAPTER 18

Fast-forward ten years, and Tia and Grace, armed with International Business and Marketing degrees, are on the team to market Sean/a's story with compassionate understanding and popular social media analytics wherewithal. Cecile is still heading up business and marketing strategy for Sean/a's book, and Hilary and Haley are still part of photo shoots, events, representation, and branding. Sean/a's team. Comprising dear old friends and family who have always believed in and been inspired by her spirit of overcoming, along with some new faces.

I can just hear her now saying, "Bless!" and "Praise!" in the way only Sean/a can—full embodiment, arms outstretched. To truly know Sean/a is to love her. I cannot imagine my life without Sean/a's daily texts and insights regarding the human condition.

A prescient friend of mine, Arielle, asked whether Sean/a might be a guru to me. I've run that question up and down my soul. As far as a leader and teacher pointing the way toward growth—both personal and collective—absolutely, yes. She has no dogma or insistence on adopting a systematic way of thinking; rather, her essential way of being in the world inspires me in its contagious, exuberant, communal focus.

It has become hard to separate her lived coaching from my own embodied sense of universal truths. Her formidable energy has informed my outlook on humanity and, most importantly, on the power of community. Generosity of spirit flows mutually between Sean/a and whatever community she is part of.

The boundless energy Sean/a brings to each day is astounding. She has realized that the solidarity of a group provides the strongest antidote to traumatic experiences. Thus, her deep support of the LGBTQIA community offers a shared sense of worth by reformulating which cultural constructs need changing and acknowledging the unconditional love that bonds us all together.

Sean/a has called herself the "Kim Kardashian of the formerly homeless." Her manner of fully, passionately engaging with a happy, playful-yet-grounded aura and transitioning conversation into action is contagious. The essence of life, in her book, is remaining simple yet filled with curiosity.

She sets out to deeply connect with people, free from agenda, yet these connections often act as a catalyst; whatever she is trying to accomplish is somehow brought to fruition. She is a harbinger of neighborly goodwill and an antidote to depression and loneliness.

She pulls people in for all the right reasons. She inspires and teaches, mentors, and fascinates; she gives others permission to express themselves and be comfortable in their own skin. Some have felt threatened by her "diva" mentality and suggested she should humble herself by working at a low-income job. If that were Sean/a's inclination, I am certain it would be the most populated place of business, with people drawn in by the energy she exudes.

She's been offered a job at a gallery to stand outside and draw people in, she got paid by a local restaurant to be a greeter, and she has received payment to use her image. What I have noticed is that the quintessential secret to Sean/a's success—being her fully expressive Sean/a self—magnetically attracts.

Working over 70 hours a week, without a day off, and continually running herself into the ground was what caused Sean/a to lose traction and experience that rapid descent into homelessness earlier in her life (combined with other issues, including family problems and identity struggles). It is not in her nature to do anything at half-speed, yet she agrees that rowing the boat gently is still rowing.

A measured approach can yield great dividends.

"I keep my head up and keep walking; fools hate knowledge, so I just pray," she told me. "I never had the opportunity to do something like jury duty because people were confused about me." I inferred that mental distress might interfere with her decision-making in settings such as jury duty.

"That is why I have had trouble with so many different jobs," she added. It seems that, when it came to Sean/a, chaos ensued when employers attempted to practice nondiscrimination in hiring; there appears to be at least an unconscious bias (and often it is more overt).

Attributing her complex mental struggles to PTSD from years on the streets and the confusion about her place in the world—straddling both male and female identities during a time when the world hadn't caught up to the idea—made sense to Sean/a. A possible undiagnosed disorder has also made traditional avenues of employment out of reach for Sean/a.

Despite these very real challenges to living what many would consider a "normal" or "productive" lifestyle, Sean/a's legacy of post-traumatic growth and resilience highlight how combining the proper ingredients can create a wholly meaningful existence. This can also be achieved by relational connection while being faithful to address systematic betrayal and subjugation.

Building "intercultural trust"[17] within her various communities and harnessing the natural impulse to protect one's own—whether in the Black, gay, or other communities—gives Sean/a the confidence to combat intracultural pressures that impact mental health. Solidarity and wholeness within create ripples of acceptance outward.

Understanding oneself also begets compassion and assistance. Playing to her strengths has let the sun in Sean/a's soul shine. With the discovery of technology and the myriad opportunities for connection on her own terms and her own schedule, Sean/a has spent a

---

17   Jennifer Gomez, "Cultural Betrayal Trauma Theory," jmgomez.org, 2024.

decade honing her ideas and using her skills to serve others through documenting her story.

I believe Sean/a has lived as humbly as one can, given her life on the streets. She has learned to make herself visible and respected by not dwelling on her circumstances but instead turning every misfortune into a fortune cookie—complete with a new cheerful prescription for the future. Sean/a is her own cheerleader and that, in turn, transforms the many lives lucky enough to be in her orbit.

She recharges through her spiritual connection and deep faith in God.

There is so much Sean/a in the room, yet she also makes space and defers to others graciously.

She is an incredibly cherished friend. Through steps of my journey—marriage, divorce, raising kids, and encountering health concerns, not to mention Covid—she has been every ounce as true a friend as any others in my circle. I look back at the past decade and realize that Sean/a's presence in my life has illuminated fundamental truths, some of which were hard to hide from, such as a marriage with foundational differences regarding one's role in the lives of others.

I believe that spreading grace—especially when one has had the benefit of more fortunate circumstances—is an imperative, not a question. I've come to realize, however, that my reflexive manner is not the only way this can be achieved. I give great kudos to my ex-husband for buying into my vision as long as he did and for spreading grace in his own manner, as he has touched many lives on and off the pro tennis circuit.

Sean/a also honors my daughter's soccer and educational journey and is the first to send congratulations when each new milestone is reached. She has often praised and supported Tia with texts and her unique brand of wisdom. The numerous biblical teachings she has stressed to me have inevitably worked their way into my daily feed-back to Tia—consciously or not.

I am by far a more patient parent with Sean/a's reminders that "with kids comes chaos," and laughter to follow.

My daughter, helpful and curious, yet fully absorbed in her re-lentless grind chasing elusive goals and dreams, has relished the chance to be of service with a behind-the-scenes approach. She has risen to the occasion countless times at my behest on Sean/a's behalf. I would be remiss if I didn't acknowledge the occasional "Mom, this is your deal, not mine. I'm too busy right now," followed by, "Okay, WHAT do you need me to do now?" On text this is capped off with an "lol" when she understands the nearsightedness of her vision.

I am reminded of the countless unyielding demands placed upon today's youth. Sean/a's life of simplicity, by contrast, affords her time for contemplation and reflection. This hard-won luxury to simply dwell in one's thoughts and possibility yields patience, forgiveness, and compassion. These virtues that Sean/a has cultivated through extreme hardship are her timeless, most soulful rewards for enduring and surviving the unthinkable.

If only today's youth could understand that the light at the end of the struggle is glorious. Breaking open to the quintessential truths IS the prize they are seeking.

In watching Sean/a's unfolding journey, I believe my daughter has come to understand the intangible reward of knowing one has the power to dramatically alter the trajectory of a human life, often by kindness and willingness alone. This has been a transformative realization. Slowing down to take another's perspective and holding space for connection makes all the difference, and that is the golden shift in perspective. The rewards are much more fulfilling than one's GPA or a million likes on Instagram!

Ten years of connection with Sean/a has redirected me more powerfully to the living, breathing community composed of fascinating people and their various stories.

I've always been social and an inherent lover of people. From cheer captain, homecoming queen in high school (a fact I don't commonly share) to psychologist. People. Growth. Encouragement. Support. It's what I love. But Sean/a takes this to a level that challenges even my off-the-charts extroversion. A whole new scale would need to be invented to measure hers.

Sean/a lives and breathes her idealism. A voracious learner, seeing life itself as a source of renewal, she invites people who feel marginalized to create an inner sense of belonging by embracing the way they are different. Her fresh and positive mindset, sense of awe and wonder, levity and depth at appropriate moments, and intention to live life in the miraculous all act as a model to aspire to and tether oneself.

Sean/a creates and imagines an ever-expanding and uplifting spiral. When she feels alone, for example, she casts her net far and wide and eventually finds she couldn't possibly be lonely when she is connected to all of humanity.

In La Jolla, she was an icon—the jewel in the jewel. In our community, she learned that her years of service, connecting, working, sports, and friendships ran deep, and that people would rally behind her in her time of need (as she had done behind the scenes for so many).

Living in Palm Springs has taught her about being a different kind of contributing member of the community. She has learned about mutuality in a place she didn't live in as marginalized or homeless. Sean/a channels her teaching and coaching energy into the community.

Sean/a did her best to create a new story and new beginning for herself in Palm Springs, adding to its vibrant, accepting energy. But there are times she misses the friends and community of La Jolla, which she enjoyed for decades.

CHAPTER 18

When Sean/a returned to Palm Springs after her spectacular trip to New York, she expressed, "My brain and feet miss that place already, but it's totally different having a place to come home to; I loved returning to my apartment. I feel light on my feet, it seems brand-new again."

Everywhere she goes, she spreads cheer and goodwill and amazes me with her ability to adapt and explore. Yet no matter where she finds herself, Sean/a feels increasingly more at home. This was a battle hard-won, a long time in coming, and she honors every moment of life feeling at home in her own skin.

Her exuberance of shining brightly and standing bravely as who she is was apparent during the most recent photo shoots. Two women named Kim—both freelance photographers who offered to do separate photo shoots with Sean/a—did a phenomenal job. The photo shoots ended up being great fun.

Kim H. spent hours on two different occasions following Sean/a around her old haunts—the rec center, the basketball court, the beach, and La Valencia. Everywhere, she had left spiritual footprints. Kim U. picked up where we left off: filming in the desert, Newport, Laguna, and full circle back to La Jolla. The nonlinguistic photographic testimony emanating from Sean/a's body language, gestures, and posture in the reflective, artistic poses in the photos conveys deep truth regarding her struggle, liberation, and transcendence.

One of her photographers described Sean/a as the "light spot" in her weeks because no matter how hard the day had been, Sean/a would walk by in her colorful outfits with a broad smile on her face and make it seem like all was well in the world.

If Sean/a could get through the numerous obstacles facing her each day with optimism and joy, then everyone else could as well. I have a smile on my face picturing Sean/a's extroverted, hip persona exclaiming, "Praise!" or "Girrrrrlllll, you should've been there."

289

Both Sean/a and I enjoyed our now 40th high school reunions this past September, hers in Las Vegas and mine in Minnesota. As we compared notes afterward, we were fascinated to realize there was so much overlap—with wonderful turnouts—and we both felt deep-hearted joy that we were still alive and healthy and able to take part in this time of reconnecting.

The theme for both of us definitely centered around gratitude and a deep witnessing of life's journeys.

It is incredible to me that Sean/a—who had transferred her senior year—had made such an impact on her class. After so many years being disconnected from the group, she has re-emerged as a very thoughtful and contributing member of the class of 1984 once again. She is in regular touch with the planning committee and has notably kept close contact with her friend Butch, who has been as kind and gracious as family.

Since her first attended reunion in her purple wig five years ago, she has fully immersed herself in alumni affairs and events. No more shock value as a defense against rejection. Comfort in her own skin and authenticity is the new look.

It is heartening to compare notes and recognize the depth of goodwill and good cheer at our age and to celebrate these milestones together.

I absolutely loved the photos Sean/a sent me in her gorgeous, sophisticated, and naturally beautiful wig, flats, and dress. She looked like a completely different woman from five years prior. It almost brought tears to my eyes, recognizing how she'd grown into feeling completely comfortable in her skin and a part of the group. Gone was the trepidation that had plagued her five years ago.

Deep belonging. It showed in every photo.

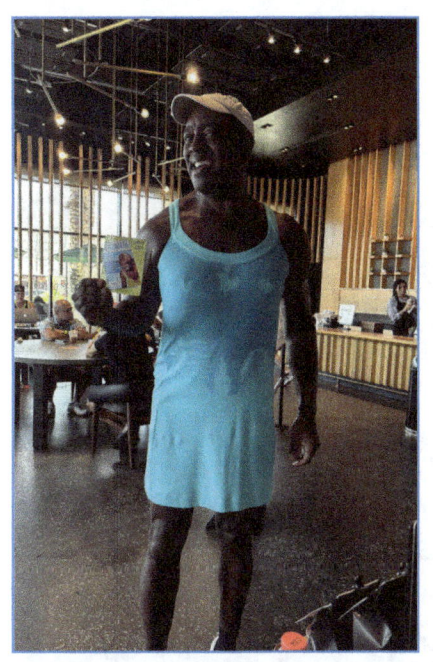

CHAPTER 19

Retracing Early Steps

"It is so important to 'love thy neighbor' and extend a helping hand or kind word because these connections become reconnections one day. Life brings you back around to these places."

~ Sean/a

For some time, Sean/a had expressed a fervent desire to retrace her early years growing up in Columbia, Maryland, where she had lived until the age of ten when the family had moved to Northglenn, Colorado. We decided to combine it with a trip to Washington, DC, for some advocacy inspiration. The nation's capital was teeming with possibility and strong emotions with the 2024 presidential election only weeks away.

I (more than Sean/a) was getting riled up. I was firmly aligned with one candidate in the upcoming election while Sean/a showed herself as more neutral, trying to extol the values from each while distancing herself from radical agendas on either side. I shouldn't have been surprised that Sean/a expressed her skill for rising above in this way instead of stressing out about something so clearly beyond our control.

Sean/a, again taking everything in stride, offered up measured doses of philosophical insights as we toured DC on our Hop-On-Hop-Off bus, which she had noticed was generously offered by our hotel concierge. Although both my daughter and I had spent our collegiate years in the area, neither of us had previously availed ourselves of this insightful and pleasurable opportunity.

As I watched Sean/a plugged into her headset with thoughtful concentration and admiration for the nation's imposing edifices, absorbing and digesting so much historical information, I was filled with an immense appreciation for her intelligent and inquisitive nature. I could readily understand how she had always been interested in education and teaching as a profession.

Ever a loyal watch of the Palm Springs and La Jolla police departments, Sean/a was enthralled with the DC Secret Service and insisted on taking multiple photos for her friends in the Palm Springs PD.

I silently noted an interesting parallel. Riding in the car with her on this trip had prompted many moments of brief "conversations" between her and her internal others. As she would talk to her voices sternly but politely, "Ma'am, please, not now," and "Sir, I know, yes," I felt her internal secret police was on endless watch lest we make any wrong moves.

After passing through upscale Georgetown and seeing a swath of tourists, it was especially poignant witnessing the many homeless encampments from the vantage point of a visitor on vacation. I was reminded that one of the key features of surviving with her joy and optimism intact is Sean/a's ability to adapt to whatever situation she faced. Her outfits in D.C. were colorful and expressive. She often wore a pink miniskirt and baseball hat, though she was well aware that conservative businessmen and tourists alike were giving her more than a second glance.

We only heard one rude comment from a teenage girl. Ironically, it took place right outside the White House. She and her mom were dressed in traditional religious attire from a non-Western country, and I remarked to Sean/a that her looks may have been more curiosity as to how Sean/a could express such personal freedom publicly rather than judgment. Sean/a wasn't convinced.

She had heard that the pastor from her online church was touring the Museum of the Bible in DC that week. So, next on the agenda—aside from all the usual sightseeing and photo-taking near the White House—she decided we should visit that museum. She wanted to honor the way that faith had played such a vital role in her formative years and gotten her through her toughest moments living homeless.

As we entered the Museum of the Bible, it was if we were entering the Holy Land itself. It was a first for both of us—the experience of wearing virtual reality goggles to "walk through" the Holy Sites. I couldn't help marveling that not only was this a spiritually profound event we were sharing, but just ten years ago I was teaching her to text one letter at a time. Sean/a and technology were advancing at lightning speed.

We ventured through many exhibits and then stopped by the gift store, where she was drawn to items that reflected her deeply positive inclusive messages. Although Sean/a feels at home in different online churches, she takes great care not to align with all the messaging; she acknowledges the communal benefits of hope and triumph of the spirit, yet leaves political discussions at the door. A wise approach.

Sean/a was insistent that we tour two historically Black colleges and universities (HBCUs). She said that even as a child, she had been placed in predominantly white private schools and was very inspired by the idea of a university and surrounding community being all Black.

We first drove to Howard University, where the university hospital brought her to tears. "A hospital just for Black people. Do you know how important this is? The sight is overwhelming."

I took in how this affected her to her core—a validation that affirmed Black lives really mattered. She commented on the fashion and confident expressive college students around her and remarked, "I have never been around so many Black people at once. I feel at home."

After Howard, she excitedly directed us toward Morgan State University. As we drove through the sprawling campus, Sean/a said, "Taking a glance at these universities is inspiring because America cares about African Americans and education."

She also noted that she grew increasingly impatient with people who have a victim mentality; she said although of course institutionalized racism is real, there are also many myths people buy into, which keeps them oppressed. She pointed to the HBCUs as shattering those assumptions and felt very liberated by these visits. The contrast between her tiny white college in Wyoming and these much larger HBCUs where belonging to the racial majority was a given, was stark.

"We have to see Georgetown University," she insisted next. "Your alma mater, Doc."

So, off we went. The two of us took a photo outside of the hall where my first Abnormal Psychology—now called Clinical Psychology—classes took place. I had TA'd for my mentor, the late William L. Kelly, a wonderful professor of psychology who set me on a path to understanding and connecting deeply with Sean/a forty years hence.

Although we didn't know each other then, I believe Sean/a and I were predestined to highly influence each other's lives. It was in those hallowed halls and classrooms that I first learned of dissociation and schizophrenia. Decades later, my rapt attention and fascination with those subjects translated into lived compassion and empathy for a journey theoretically far from mine, yet intertwined in spirit.

I soaked in the moment and conjured Dr. Kelly's energy and wisdom as I stood a bit incredulous at my remarkable relationship with Sean/a all these years later. Our educational, intellectual, spiritual, and communal paths converged outside of White-Gravenor Hall.

Next, we gave a passing nod to the famed Georgetown Thompson basketball arena, recalling my student days in 1984–1985 with Patrick Ewing and the championships. There is no other person I would've enjoyed the experience with more than my appreciative companion, Sean/a, a sports enthusiast who was always uniquely present in each moment.

We continued to make our way through DC and eventually drove past Arlington Cemetery. Sean/a turned to me with a somber look on her usually joyful face. "Doc, I feel a chill. I can just feel all of these souls." As a proud, honorably discharged vet, she took time to absorb the sanctity of place.

On our drive out of DC toward her early childhood home in Columbia, Maryland, Sean/a began to verbally process her initial trepidation, which had turned to thrill in the nation's capital. She had feared being overwhelmed by early memories of relatives on her biological father's side; however, after a while, she started sharing funny, loving memories of her paternal grandmother—Grandma Boo Boo—with whom she'd enjoyed a loving relationship before her parents' divorce.

As we headed down the highway, lined on both sides with brilliant fall foliage, Sean/a's stress seemed to melt away. So many trees, so many colors, wholly unlike the desert and reminiscent of her childhood. We checked into the Merriweather Lakehouse Hotel, which felt like an expansive cabin escape with its gorgeous lake nearby. Sean/a immediately embarked on a mood-walk therapy session.

After she had refreshed, we embarked upon retracing her childhood steps. First stop, the house she had grown up in. As we slowly drove down a street called Lucky Penny Lane, she called out suddenly, "Stop, this is the place." I slowed the vehicle as she continued narrating the place from her memory of decades earlier.

"It didn't used to have that garage, but there's a long driveway behind it with another home." Sure enough, as we approached, there it was, hidden from view just as she said.

"Homes built back in the day were smart," Sean/a observed. "They were built right next door to each other so if family came over, you didn't feel alone. Today with suburbs, we are all so spread out."

As she proceeded to tell me stories of the neighbors and cousins living nearby, a man emerged from the house. Sean/a introduced herself and explained her family were the owners of the home over 40 years earlier. All the dates lined up, and they got into a lively exchange about where Sean/a's room and her sister's had been.

Much goodwill was left on that doorstep.

Sean/a kept saying, "I can't believe it. Columbia, Maryland. My childhood home. I never thought I'd see it again." Moments like these drew a well of emotion and one million percent gratified the deepest part of my being. Next, we were retracing her educational history from elementary school through to the beginning of middle school when they moved to Northglenn, Colorado, for Jesse's job as a pastor.

As we pulled up to Phelps Luck Elementary, Sean/a looked around, noting that although much had changed, the essentials had stayed the same. The demographic of Columbia—now predominantly affluent African Americans—had been mostly Caucasian in her formative years. She described her parents as having had the vision to enroll them as kids in the best schools regardless of their social status. After a photo outside of Longfellow School, where she'd attended briefly, we ventured on.

Our next stop, in the suburbs of Ilchester, took us to the lush grounds of the private school she and her sister had attended.

"We had to take a very long bus ride. We were the first to be picked up and the last to be dropped off, it was that far," she explained as we approached a positively charming school nestled among winding wooded country roads. I noted many "no trespassing" signs leading into the place. The immense buildings were in brownstone architectural style, and the grounds were green, well-trimmed, and immaculate.

Sean/a described the cranberry tie and gray pants uniforms she wore at Holy Trinity School, and relayed how her favorite teacher had been her gym teacher, whose career she wanted to emulate one day. Recalling her teachers—Sister Katherine in second grade and Mrs. Kramer in third grade—then reminded her of friendships she'd formed in this place of nurturing and growth.

"Every Wednesday, we had chocolate milk," she recalled, "and we went to the Smithsonian Institute on field trips." Out of nowhere, a groundskeeper appeared. He introduced himself as the gym teacher. Of course, a long conversation ensued between him and Sean/a. I observed Sean/a in her pink miniskirt, talking and laughing as if there were no barriers between them.

Perhaps there weren't.

~ ~ ~

On our way to the train station, which would take her on a long-promised follow-up visit to New York City, we spent a few hours in Baltimore, visiting Fells Point, the Inner Harbor, and Johns Hopkins University, where my daughter was currently playing on the soccer team while pursuing her master's degree.

Sean/a felt a special kinship there, since the JHU hospital had established the first gender-affirming surgery clinic in the US in our birth year, 1966. Additionally, their center for transgender and gender-expansive health and gender affirmations services made her feel especially welcomed and comfortable.

She bought a JHU sweater to remind herself that in the highly prestigious open-minded center of learning, she was not an outsider. She felt embraced, welcomed, and normalized.

"My sister was born in DC, not far from here," Sean/a observed as we continued on. She gave a silent nod of gratitude for Robin's safe birth. The disparity between rich and poor varied block by block in the charming yet sometimes violent city of Baltimore.

As we meandered through the city toward the train station, detouring through what was googled to be a LGBTQIA-friendly area, Sean/a commented, "I'm still incredulous that Miss Maryland won the pageant as a beautiful transgendered woman." She added, "Inner beauty prevails and overcomes all obstacles."

I said goodbye to Sean/a as she boarded a train to NYC, armed with shopping money, excitement, gratitude, and a warm coat for the brisk weather.

~ ~ ~

After our journey to DC, the first trip in which I had actually accompanied her in person, I had the opportunity to talk with Sean/a's sister at length about the places we had visited. Sean/a related how special her childhood had been to her, and I shared with Robin what a privilege it had been to witness her recollections of the powerful and palpable familial love and guidance, especially educationally, she had received from her mom and Jesse.

As we spoke, Robin corroborated addresses and schools and chimed in with Sean/a's sentiment that they had grown up feeling privileged. From visits with grandparents and cousins nearby, ample friendships, and even enjoying popularity at predominantly white, elite schools, Robin filled in some of the gaps and validated many of Sean/a's sentiments.

At the same time, stories regarding her father's side of the family remained vague and appeared a bit untouchable. I didn't pry, ever mindful of the importance of respecting boundaries and both personal and family privacy. She confirmed that they had had a loving relationship with their grandmother, whom they called Grandma Boo Boo, until they moved away from Maryland.

"It seems like your family was ahead of the curve in seeking educational opportunities," I observed.

"Yes, we wanted for nothing," Robin agreed. "Everyone was always welcomed, and guidance and love were given out freely."

In general, her family had vision and strove to fit in and flourish. Education and God were the cornerstones, which remain for both surviving siblings to this day.

"I hope you don't mind my mentioning this," I said, "but it seemed to perplex Sean/a why the two of you were so close as children, and yet as adults, it was like your relationship had fragmented."

Robin let out a sigh. "There are a couple of reasons she might feel that way." She told me about when Sean/a was living in San Diego, as Sean at the time, and had developed a close friendship with a couple whose children Sean had been nannying.

"I was always my little brother's keeper," Robin said. "Well, I gave a stern talking to the man because I felt like Sean was being exploited. I think that was one thing that caused some misunderstanding." Sean/a had enjoyed taking care of those kids, but there was also confusion in that relationship, which might have exacerbated her identity crisis at the time.

"Why, with so many lost years, did no one file a missing person report or try to look for Sean/a in earnest?" I asked. I immediately regretted the question, hearing her emotional response on the other end of the line.

She explained how she was in the middle of a truly stressful season of life, with raising her kids—a sentiment I completely understand. Parenting is no joke, and motherhood is a challenge unlike any other.

"Our stepfather, Jesse, actually hired a private investigator."

"Really?" It was the first time I'd heard about this.

"Eventually, the PI reported that he had found Sean, but with the tone of Jesse's response, it was along the lines of 'I know Sean is alive, but don't ask too many questions.'"

I wasn't sure what to make of this, and Robin didn't have any further information. Jesse had since passed away, and whatever knowledge he had learned had gone with him.

"Was there a specific event or falling out?" I asked.

"There was one time I got worked up when Sean visited for Christmas, years ago," Robin said. "He came out of the room dressed very flamboyantly. It was like a trigger, bringing back memories of our other brother, who had passed away from AIDS. I was afraid Sean was going to head down that same road."

"What happened?" I pressed.

"I remember yelling, telling Sean he was not allowed to dress like that around my children. I guess I was extra-cautious with my boundaries."

I understood Robin's concern. It is hard to imagine the myriad responsibilities she was juggling at the time, as well as being a parental figure to her sibling after their mother and brother passed.

Looking back on the situation, I also realize the silencing of Sean/a's essential self at that time must have been triggering, which eventually

304

resulted in her leaving in a fit of emotion. Although she rarely spoke much about that time in her life, some aspects of it must have affected her deeply. Over time, those wounds healed in her ongoing journey.

I reflected on the bonding (and very enlightening) trip we had just taken together. Although I had planned many trips for her in the past, this was the first time we had traveled and explored new sights together with real-time processing and witnessing. I felt grateful for the experience.

It seemed natural how smoothly we alternately took the lead, and I appreciated how she navigated potentially awkward social situations deftly, even in her pink miniskirt alongside men and women in suits. She made friends with everyone along the way, striking up conversations and answering numerous questions from ever-curious fellow tourists.

Sean/a showed great empathy for the homeless; seeing the plight of the unhoused during our travels highlighted her current housed status as something she had continual appreciation for. Ironically, she was headed to NYC, Fifth Avenue shopping, a horse-and-carriage ride through Central Park, and another fascinating adventure in Times Square. How things had changed in her life!

She told me that she checked into the "W" hotel in Times Square and received a very warm welcome, with congratulatory champagne, once she told them she'd finished our book. After that, she promptly took advantage of the free boat tour to Lady Liberty. Sean/a sent me a text and photo.

"Doc, check this out! I'm on a yacht tour to emancipation."

In the five years since her last visit to New York City, a mature Sean/a had emerged—a woman comfortable in her own skin who'd earned her right to walk with her head high, carrying her own torch.

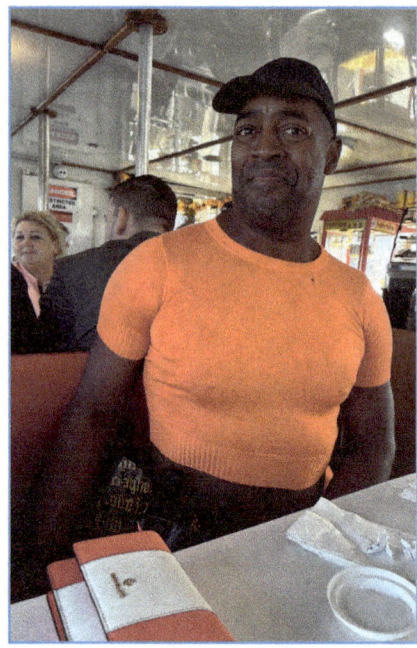

CHAPTER 20

Hope for the Future

"Staying true to my ethical principles makes me content and satisfied. Mother Teresa did incredible things. If people thought she was somewhat grandiose for wanting to go out and help all those sick people, the reality is what she did was nothing short of amazing. I feel like I can take that as motivation and say, 'I can do the right things.'"

~ Sean/a

O n our last day at the lakeside hotel in Maryland, Sean/a invited me to join her after-dinner walk. It had been years since I had gone on a mood-walk therapy excursion with Sean/a.

As we trekked around the lake, she said, "I'm going to remember this place." She closed her eyes and inhaled deeply. "It's a memory I'll come back to and use to calm myself when I want to feel a sense of tranquility and nature. 'The Lake.'"

She smiled. "I love the desert; it's my home now, but this reminds me of who I once was. Sometimes it's good to remember." We continued, enjoying the refreshing, crisp fall air. Wildlife abounded—deer, rabbits, and yes, squirrels.

Before long, we found ourselves deep in the swampy woodlands.

"Doc, this is kinda scary. It's so dark with no city lights." Somehow, even with her imposing six-foot-five presence, ironically and metaphorically, I felt I could protect her from the wayward wildlife. As so many animals were getting ready for hibernation, Sean/a had completely emerged from hers.

Awake. Aware. And hungry to experience all that life has yet to offer.

I envision the future full of hope and newfound security while advocating together for those whose lives need a little Sean/a-style resilience, perseverance, and perspective. The sky is the limit when it comes to her possibilities. As Tina Turner—her idealized "mom"—would likely proudly exclaim, "Keep it rolling, Sean/a."

~ ~ ~

Sean/a seeks to follow the Golden Rule, considering others in everything she does. During the pandemic, she began greeting me with the phrase, "I hope your igloo, your family is doing well." She still says that from time to time, with true concern about the "igloos" of every person she interacts with.

Her work against bullying as a "street prophet for kindness" has transformed many an unpalatable circumstance and has taught compelling lessons to those willing to open their hearts and minds. Sean/a impels people to confront their shadows by her very—seemingly controversial—existence. She appears to possess a sixth sense in attracting those who most need to reorganize their previously held assumptions and constructs.

Sean/a's problem-solving acuity and intuitive flashes of on-the-spot insight often foster an increase in spiritual wisdom—a state of being that transpersonal psychologists and cultural anthropologists recognize as shamanic in nature. Some validate the idea of shamanic soul retrieval and how, in the presence of Sean/a, they felt reconnected to their own deep knowing and a rewelcoming of disowned parts of themselves.

It has been so very heartening, a decade later, when I reflect on the sense of belonging with purpose that has informed my relationship with Sean/a. This power has also been true in regard to my deep friendships with my Soul Wise Coaching (now Soul Wise Solutions) cofounders, Hilary and Cecile. We are all still the closest of friends, and now that we have emerged "empty nesters," we have once again rallied our strengths around Sean/a.

Hilary recently expressed, "Sean/a's indomitable spirit against all odds, as the ambassador of La Jolla, deeply inspired me. I so admire Sean/a's positivity, humility, and larger-than-life presence." She told me, "Sean/a has such an immense sense of gratitude and generosity, it's insane." Hilary's daughter, Haley, a true Sean/a fan, also lovingly shares Sean/a's all-inclusive mindset.

Cecile has gotten on board with executive coaching sessions as a vital part of launching Sean/a's book project forward. As always, Hilary and Cecile jump in where they are needed and where their valuable skills can help Sean/a the most. Most importantly, they provide emotional support, a buffer of love and comfort, and a never-wavering attitude of "we've got this."

The three of us are once again demonstrating the power of friendship as the foundational bedrock from which anything is possible. In the ensuing years from our first Shelter for Shauna campaign, each of us has faced many personal challenges. Throughout it all, we have maintained a singular mission: to be there for one another, whatever it takes. I firmly believe this loyal commitment has made all the difference when each of us was navigating uncharted, sometimes rough, waters. We have all grown immensely and become a safe harbor for each other during life's unexpected storms.

Sean/a and Soul Wise have evolved both personally and together. We share an inclusive sensibility in our goal of helping women in various kinds of transitions in life. Ironically, although Sean/a was the quintessential example of a woman in transition, she immediately made us realize that she could teach and coach us in the art of embracing change ... viewing it as the quest unto itself.

Sean/a reminded us in many little ways to depend upon the spiritual guidance that was always within our reach. The wisdom of her soul nudged us toward becoming more truly "soul wise."

~ ~ ~

Recently, Sean/a remarked that she has moved into healing. Even though it is lonely at the top, she says she still would've chosen most of her journey because she has grown to love her life more than her wildest dreams. And it all started with fully accepting the core of herself.

People who have had near-death experiences have stated that there are light beings who take on human form; these spiritually enlightened ones come down to this plane to get us centered. Sean/a could very well be one of these light beings. She maintains positive illusions versus delusions, preferring to live in the sense of life as it should be and people as they could be. As we embrace such possibilities, I believe we can awaken each other collectively to a God consciousness.

Society's rules often result in usurping of will and conquering of spirit, which only serves to divide us against ourselves. Meaningful, positive experiences can prevail as the antidote to distorted self-concept and negative cognitions that arise during stressful situations. Sean/a serves as an example of allegiance to a higher law that reflects and espouses integration, wholeness, self-respect, and self-actualization.

CHAPTER 20

Sean/a's integration of the past manifested her present success.

In La Jolla, as she was constantly on the move, interacting with others, this book was being written step by literal step. On a recent trip back to La Jolla, I tasked Sean/a with handing out "book coming soon" fliers. She proudly dispersed them throughout the large village community. Not only did she feel legitimized, a decade later, that the elusive book project had finally come to fruition, but it became an icebreaker to engage in conversation and an invitation to go visit old friends.

Sean/a delighted in the opportunity to market her story all around San Diego. Gaining respite from the scorching, record-breaking (123 degree!) desert heat, she logged first 17, then 20 miles of daily walks back to back at the seaside.

Back in Palm Springs, Sean/a's memoir took on a tone of reflection. A high level of mental healing and identity assimilation took place during those daily half-marathons of mood-walk therapy. (I'm pretty sure she outwalked Forrest Gump. As of this writing, Seana has completed almost 750 days toward her goal of 10 to 15 miles DAILY.) As she hands out cards at her local Starbucks and on her walks, she explains how she came to the desert to truly find herself.

Spending the past ten years living, remembering, telling, and writing her story has proudly put another huge achievement on Sean/a's resume. Upon receipt of her copy of the working manuscript, she excitedly exclaimed, "Doc, I'm an author. I'm an AUTHOR!"

~ ~ ~

Sean/a's life lived with courage and determination, passion and enthusiasm, wisdom and knowledge, gratitude, and love, is a direct result of having entered and emerged from the abyss. As she re-engaged with the world from the safety of her apartment, she exhibited post-traumatic growth. As Sean/a's outer world transformed, she then did some long-overdue internal housekeeping.

Her experience of life was clearly being guided by higher forces that appeared to confer significant advantages. Her enhanced spiritual matrix goes beyond neural connections. It infuses mentally broadening experiences that flow from a greater Source. The quantum energies occupying her mental field allow for communion with that which is ineffable yet is the center of all-being and omniscient.

Sean/a appears aglow when her luminescence is honored. Her whole being portrays a healthy, balanced, mature acceptance of her life's circumstances. Along the way, she has learned and developed coping skills such as accountability, which is related to sense, order, and productivity. A big part of this accountability comes through relationships, in community.

Dependency and intimacy help meet the needs each of us has to feel unique. Helping each other illuminate the path during challenging times, or struggling together in the darkness, are perhaps the kindest spiritual gestures we can offer each other. This is what community means to Sean/a.

Sean/a is a joiner, a friend, an advocate, a seer, a prophet, a generous spirit, and most importantly, a humanitarian. She has become transfigured in the way she manifests to the world, and her evolution as Sean/a has only further illuminated her inherent glow.

Interestingly, those who have had spiritually transformative experiences (and even near-death experiences) often speak of feeling a special importance or destiny, a favor from God, a sense of the preciousness of life and a more positive attitude. To be in Sean/a's presence, interacting with her aura, I feel something of the same. She conveys a deep sense of understanding universal truths, illuminating insights, and tranquility, almost through spiritual osmosis.

322

Continually evolving, she appears to be querying, "How would I want the world to be different because I lived in it?" but also "Where can I break the mold and the rules, and where do I adhere to some sort of convention?" Like a child full of boundless curiosity, she is always (sometimes unintentionally) pushing the limits around her to find where her own boundaries lie.

An open-hearted, loving stance is what she brings forth, both virtually and in real life. Those who gravitate toward her feel their lives immeasurably touched and enriched. They surrender to her cosmic teaching and unclutter their internal inboxes, if only for a fleeting "Sean/a moment" of transcendent awareness.

Sean/a doesn't allow herself to be pulled into others' agendas; she stays strongly rooted in herself, with God as her guide. She firmly believes in the power of remaining fully centered and brings every ounce of herself to each moment.

~ ~ ~

Symbols and myths have great relevance for mankind; valuing these eternal icons trace the mind's development and invite dialogue into the repressed components of the wounded spirit.

Sean/a carries within her deep Christian teachings, stating, "I spent a lot of time listening to my stepfather Jesse, a pastor, teach as well as listening to contemporary Christian radio. That audial learning never really goes away; it is deeply ingrained with who I am."

She attends a virtual church every week with her old congregation in El Cajon and is active in the community of parishioners. Her faith comes into play in observations she regularly makes, such as, "I don't think God was playing games; I think I was put in this very community for a reason."

When each of us authentically lives true to our nature and essential goodness, the vibrant, dynamic energy that accompanies such daring is unlimited in potential. As such, we are liberated to create a life of our own choosing and in accordance with spiritual principles that uplift and carry us through.

This is what I have seen Sean/a accomplish in my time of knowing her. This is what she has the unique ability to inspire in others as well.

~ ~ ~

Today, Sean/a's vision is simple. She told me, "My hope for the future is to find happiness and security in a home, a financial adviser, and an island all to myself."

Then she laughed loudly, causing me to join in. "Somehow I don't think you'll be alone for long," I said.

"But seriously, I hope for good health to be able to enjoy the rest of my life here on earth. I'll try my hardest to make my communities safe for all, even for those who have trouble understanding or who struggle with forgiveness and acceptance. I have faith and I have patience."

Her advice to all is short and sweet: "Seek solutions. Be an advocate, be a friend. Pay it forward. Pray."

This has never been a story where the main character ends up a sports legend or concerns a well-known cultural figure rising to a career peak. It is a story of community and relationship, and for Sean/a, it is a story that is still advancing.

Each new day is one of moving forward, presenting more possibilities and opportunities to share her positivity and life's wonders with others.

Her life has meaning. She embraces each day and cherishes it and reiterates from the beginning, "My dignity is restored."

Sean/a will continue raising her voice on every platform available to inspire others and as a call to action for nondiscrimination, safety, health, peace, harmony, understanding, and equal rights for all. Her vision also includes more travel and a home to call her own.

CHAPTER 20

May we wish her well on this continued journey and walk proudly alongside her in joy and faith that the rights of those who feel
invisible will be honored and that their souls will feel uplifted.

We are not so different after all. Sean/a is all of us.

I would say, using Tina's words, she's "SIMPLY THE BEST."

"My greatest beauty secret is being happy with myself. I believe that a lot of how you look is to do with how you feel about yourself and your life. Happiness is the greatest beauty secret."

Tina Turner

ACKNOWLEDGMENTS

Kirsten:

My gratitude to all who have helped in the journey of writing this book knows no bounds.

To my ever-supportive parents, you model generosity of spirit in all that you do. Even when you didn't understand what path I was taking, you rallied behind me, lending your strength. Dad (Alfred), as my first editor, your feedback was invaluable, necessarily propelling the story forward. Mom (Ingrid), I am grateful for your copy editing and inquisitive comments, inspiring me to dig deeper and offer clarifications. None of this could've come to fruition without your endless love, patience, and support.

Lars, my dear brother, thank you for your offering of intellectual and humanitarian guidance. Your Oxford education came in handy when I needed clarification on a topic. You never wavered in your belief in the project (or in me). To my creative, caring sister-in-law Jacqui, my nieces Shanti and Leia, and my nephew Lukas, you kept me grounded and happy throughout our many travels and adventures wherein I would share fun Sean/a texts and excerpts, bringing us all joy.

Most importantly, my heartfelt gratitude goes out to my daughter, Tia, who has lived this story alongside me since she was 13. Over the years she has become an incredible advocate and researcher, coordinator, and marketer on Sean/a's behalf. Tia, your work ethic and commitment to your passion is beyond inspirational. The kids you've coached and mentored along the way—always teaching that wellness and mental health are paramount—are incredibly fortunate to have you as their champion. You give me hope for the future as you continue to balance it all! Although my life's choices and projects have necessarily included you even when you had no idea what your mom was doing, you've been the best co-captain of our little team. I couldn't have asked for a better daughter. Thank you, Goose.

How can I begin to thank my Publishing Partner turned most supportive friend, Bethany Kelly? You have tirelessly worked with me with the patience of a saint for the past eight years. There are no words for the bedrock of support and unyielding faith in this project, Sean/a, and me that you continue to have. I am forever in your debt. Your ideas and expertise are unmatched in their heartfelt conviction and execution. From start to finish, you got me through the swirling of ideas, interviews, transcripts, and lived experience by your caring and professionalism. It was definitely synchronicity that brought you and me together on this meaningful journey. Thanks also to your amazing team, designer Stefan Merour and proofreader Frank Steele.

Bonita Jewel, my official editor, you were tasked with coaching a clinician to become a storyteller, and you opened my eyes to the power of dialogue and narrative. You truly rescued this manuscript, incorporating feedback while staying true to the original text and voice. Your helpful guidance and fresh enthusiasm made me trust you to bring out the best in Sean/a's story. I'm grateful beyond measure.

I would also like to thank Jon Curzon with Jericho Writers' editing services in the UK. Your careful and detailed reading and heartfelt engagement with the manuscript provided valuable insights which, coupled with your curiosity regarding Sean/a's essential being, spurred the next iteration of the work on to its fullest potential.

Lou C. and Anthony Guerreri, your assistance in helping Sean/a secure housing was a godsend. Thank you for your faith in Sean/a!

Tyler Korda, I appreciate the workouts, training, and your endless patience. As I bounced around ideas, you kept me rooted in strength.

Deep gratitude to Johnny Blackburn. Your guiding wisdom, deep love of humanity and healing as well as therapeutic insights have taught me grounded presence coupled with heart-centered witnessing.

Kim Gibson, our endless talks and beautifying for photo shoots help me let my inner self lead the way, knowing you took care of the outer. You've had so much patience and caring for Sean/a over the years. Thank you.

Speaking of photo shoots, Kim Hoffman, your original noticing of Sean/a and validation of her person was a gigantic step in making her feel seen. Your photos of Sean/a in and around La Jolla are breathtaking.

Kim Utley, wow! Your creativity is astounding. So much fun and flair. I'll forever consider our photo days as some of the most memorable, zany adventures! I love how you were enraptured by Sean/a's spirit and did whatever it took—like blasting music in a local park or beach—to elicit the fun and laughter between us.

Claudia Grasso, thank you for the warm winter clothing and making sure Sean/a stayed cozy and fashionably dignified as well as your lifelong advocacy for the oppressed.

Andrea Leone, thank you for the original book design draft, for being a great business consultant and friend throughout the years, and for your organizational skills and content—which you kept safe for nine years!

Christy Woodrow, you've heard me share about Sean/a since our friendship began, and I couldn't think of anyone more loyal and committed to better guide the website and future promotional content.

Chris del Muro, your thoughtful attention to detail is so very appreciated as you've diligently made your way through this manuscript and helped in all creative aspects, with huge respect and curiosity for Sean/a's story.

Carlos Vasquez, you inspire with your emotional intelligence and capacity for heartfelt connection. Thanks for helping keep me centered and healthy with wellness coaching and cooking sessions which nourish body, mind, and Spirit.

Brian Hilliard and Arielle Ford, thank you for the heartfelt difference you've made in the lives of many with your emphasis on love and soul. You came to Sean/a's aid immediately and generously. Your experienced eyes and deep wisdom, insights, and recommendations for the manuscript have made this book infinitely better. Your guidance, wisdom, and patient counsel steered me toward a bigger vision for the work. Lastly, your referral to Jericho and the reminder that "you can't f**k this up" (in a good way) was very much taken to heart. Our community is infinitely blessed to have you both so invested in humanity.

Vivian Glyck and Mike Koenigs, thank you for the brainstorms and ideas regarding this book's title. Clearly, you've left a legacy of compassion in your work to help those who have been marginalized.

Sarah Tipple, you are Sean/a's financial angel. You taught her so much by being willing to take the time to selflessly answer our call for help, and your expertise and manner have impacted her daily. We are exceedingly grateful.

Robin Wade, your artwork to honor Sean/a and the bracelets you lovingly created and donated on behalf of our fundraiser are yet more examples of how you infuse goodness and healing through your art to the global community. Your talent is only outdone by your heart.

Laura Halferty, I appreciate your expert legal guidance and heart, coupled with your willingness to lend a helping hand to those who have been systemically marginalized.

ACKNOWLEDGMENTS

Joel Leviton, Ethan Mark, and the Stinson team, your expert and compassionate legal guidance protecting Sean/a's intellectual property is paramount to the trust and safety of this project.

Renee Kohn, you rallied, rallied, and then rallied some more, always looking for ways to move our story along. Your spiritually infused energy and talent radiate a million miles. Thank you for guiding our media coaching and using your comedic and therapeutic skills in the service of this project and our heartwarming friendship.

The patience award goes to ... James Jack for your steady presence and knowing that the kids and Sean/a were the priority. Your contribution behind the scenes in keeping the household running is admired.

Kim Hoelmenn, my best friend of fifty years, we've been through it all together. No topic or life choice was ever too much for your overflowing heart to grapple with. Your fortitude and determination to walk through this life with laughter, regardless of personal trials, elicits much admiration. I'm forever in awe of you.

Steve Carlson, thanks for being a supporter of all those who have had a housing crisis. Your many years in the field and as an expert psychologist with a Christ-centered heart has blessed many.

Aaron Hoff, you lend your strength and backbone, as well as your carefully honed rational-emotive balance to make people feel they have a true friend. Sean/a is relentless in her gratitude for your time and honoring of her being on her trip "home" to Colorado.

My SOUL SISTERS—Hilary, Cecile, and Alison—true friends are called to act when the chips are down, and you heeded that call magnificently. Your faithful "We've got you" made ALL the difference in giving me the courage to keep going. You showed up for Sean/a and me in countless, life-changing ways. No matter the obstacle, I knew we would get through it TOGETHER. We started in the now and it was Plan A all the way. Our souls evolved TOGETHER. I've never felt such belonging and support.

Hil, you make everything organized and check all the boxes. Thanks for graciously attending to every detail with love and brilliant creativity. Your heart for Sean/a is truly beautiful. Alison, our lovely, thanks for your fun-loving self, jumping in wherever and whenever needed and making sure we always had tea, scones, great music and festivity, as well as philosophical advice and wonderful hugs.

Dearest Cecile, whether near or far, I can count on you to bring the most giant, stable, secure heart to the relationship. No problem is too big or small; your coaching in friendship and professionally is bar none, otherworldly in its impact. I honestly don't know how I would've gotten through the last decade without your beautiful caring. Accountability partners to the end. (We will be laughing at 100.)

Grace and Haley, thank you for your hearts filled with pure goodness.

To anyone I've left out, know you've made a fundamental impact on Sean/a's and my life.

Finally, but with utter humility, I honor Lisa and David Kaplan and their Water-Walking Foundation. Thank you, Lisa and David, for your belief in Sean/a from the beginning. Without your loving, timely, steadfast support, it is likely that none of this miraculous journey could've happened. Angels who graced all of us at the perfect time, your reach goes far and wide, fortified by your love of God. We absolutely cherish you both.

It's been an epic journey full of love, joy, and adventure. And it has only just begun!!

In loving memory of Martin, Malcolm, and Nick, whose respective love for adventure continues from beyond the veil.

ACKNOWLEDGMENTS

Sean/a:

I would like to acknowledge my gratitude first and foremost to my Lord and Savior Jesus Christ for allowing me to be a part of His plan.

Second, I would like to thank the community of La Jolla for helping me so much over the years, and the many people—too many to name—who came to my aid when I most needed it; I forever hold you in my prayers. The La Jolla Rec Center, Dr. Chen from the North Park Family Health Center, SD Health Service, Officers Morrison and the HOT team of the SD Police Dept., Bruegger's Bagels, Wells Fargo, El Pescador, La Jolla Lamborghini, my coworkers at Vons, Olga and son, Lili, Sal at Copy Cove, Maggie at Rigoberto's, your friendship and trust in me has meant so much over the years. You kept me fed and warm and made me feel human.

Trevor, my dear friend and ally, all of my teammates and coaches, my family, Oahu International Church, US Navy, Casper College Alumni Association, Christian Heritage College, Las Vegas High School, my dear old friend Steve from Colorado, my friends at the La Jolla Taco Bell, Verizon on Pearl Street, La Jolla Library, Chevron on Pearl, Staff at the *La Jolla Light*, Amanda Shotsky, Bishop's School, Jesse, Jack in the Box, CVS Pharmacy, and the La Jolla Tennis Club, Shadow Mountain Community Church, Coach John Farrell, SDUHSD, the late Coy Owens from Granite Hills High School, Martina's Taxi, and Mr. Ashton, just to name a few.

In Palm Springs, Russell and his team at Revivals, my friends at the Smoketree Ralphs Market, the Palm Springs Police Department, the Riverside County Sheriff's office, Officer Tony Pilutik, Police Chief, Mr. and Mrs. Andy Mills, and the inclusive, friendly Mayor Lisa Middleton. To the incredible DeWayne Garcia and Yvonne of Renn, thank you for welcoming me unconditionally.

Most of all, thank you, Pat Sherman, for your wonderfully compassionate articles, and your way with words, which first brought me and my story into the light.

Thank you all again for your love and support.

ABOUT THE AUTHORS

Dr. Kirsten Viola Harrison

Dr. Kirsten Viola Harrison has spent her professional career as a psychologist studying and treating trauma disorders and their sequelae. She had the opportunity to conduct research on PTSD at UCLA Neuropsychiatric Institute, as well as study at Georgetown University, Pepperdine Graduate School of Education and Psychology, Barry University, and Pacifica Graduate Institute. Kirsten's continuing education has included summers at Harvard Medical School and conferences and training in Europe, supplementing her master's degree in Biomedical Sciences.

By far the most instrumental and informative in shaping her philosophy, however, has been her direct work with trauma survivors, including near-death experiencers and those struggling with complex DID and PTSD. The creativity, passion, and will to survive the unthinkable that her clients have endured and struggled through on their healing journeys have given her life's work meaning and purpose beyond any professional training program.

It is in honor of these courageous souls that Kirsten proudly and steadfastly continues to offer her knowledge, experience, and clinical skills, in the hope that the greater good can be best served.

Kirsten is blessed to call the inspiring community of La Jolla, California, home. She can be found supporting her goalkeeper daughter's soccer career and traveling to the far reaches of the globe connecting with family and humanity. Her love of people, languages, skiing, and the ocean remind her to live in hope, gratitude, and joy.

Sean/a Smith

Sean/a Smith received a basketball scholarship to Casper College in Wyoming and eventually earned a Bachelor of Science in Physical Education from Christian Heritage College as a member of the men's basketball team. She is a certified substitute teacher and taught PE at San Dieguito High School in Encinitas, CA. Sean/a also taught aerobics and worked many years for the Boys and Girls Club.

Sean/a enjoys all things athletic, notably basketball, tennis, and walking half-marathons daily. Above all, she also faithfully attends and enjoys online church and LOVES PEOPLE.

Tina

THE TINA TURNER MUSICAL

"PREPARE TO BE ECSTATICALLY
BLOWN AWAY!"

THE DAILY BEAST

AUGUST 1-27

broadwaysf.com

I, SEAN/A

www.ingramcontent.com/pod-product-compliance
Lightning Source LLC
Chambersburg PA
CBHW071706120626

46550CB00001B/119